Ten Generations

ALSO BY CHRIS BIRCH

'Slaveowners in my family', *Genealogists' Magazine*, vol 26, no 8, December 1999

Graham
a great chief sub
with respect and gratitude
from Chris

Ten Generations

Looking backwards in time

Some glimpses of my family

Chris Birch

ST CHRISTOPHER PRESS

LONDON

2003

This edition first published in 2003 by
St Christopher Press
16 Blake Gardens, Fulham, London SW6 4QB
email: chris@sw6lon.freeserve.co.uk

2003

British Library Cataloguing in Publication Data
Birch, Chris   Ten generations : looking backwards
in time : some glimpses of my family
1.Birch, Chris - Family 2.Burt (Family) - Genealogy
3.Birch (Family) - Genealogy 4.King (Family) - Genealogy
5.St Kitts - Genealogy
I.Title II.Jepson, Chris
929.2'0972973

ISBN 0-9545721-0-6

Digitally printed in Great Britain by
Parchment (Oxford) Limited
Printworks, Crescent Road, Cowley, Oxford OX4 2PB

No man is an island, entire of it self.

John Donne

I am, in point of fact, a particularly haughty and exclusive
person, of pre-Adamite ancestral descent. You will
understand this when I tell you that I can trace my ancestry
back to a protoplasmal primordial atomic globule.
Consequently my family pride is something inconceivable.
I can't help it. I was born sneering. But I struggle
hard to overcome this defect. I mortify my pride continually.

Pooh-Bah, *The Mikado*

Only connect ....

E M Forster

With the toe bone connected
to the foot bone,
and the foot bone connected
to the ankle bone,
and the ankle bone connected
to the leg bone.
Oh mercy how they scare!

Oh those bones, oh those bones,
oh those skeleton bones.
Oh those bones, oh those bones,
oh those skeleton bones.
Oh those bones, oh those bones,
oh those bones.
Oh mercy how they scare!

Old song

This book is dedicated, with love and gratitude,
to my wife, Betty, my children, Frank and Harriet,
my daughter-in-law and my son-in-law, Ginney and Scott,
and my grandchildren, Rachel, Anne, James and Joe

Acknowledgements

My interest in my family's history began after my uncle Rufus' death with the discovery in an old tin trunk in his house in St Kitts of a Burt family tree going back to 1686. I have no idea who compiled it, but I am greatly indebted to its author. My cousin Leonard Burt greatly expanded and up-dated that tree before he was murdered in 1973, and his daughter Suzy Crenshaw kindly supplied me with a copy of Leonard's tree. Dr J M Bennett, Sir Archibald Paull Burt's biographer, has clarified a number of matters for me, and Sir Francis Burt and Simon Burt have also been very helpful with information about the Australian Burts.

As far as the Canadian Burts are concerned, I have been in regular correspondence for several years with Nora Bartman and Daphne Grove-White, who have both contributed more than they realise. Marjorie Kehoe is the principal source of what I know about the family's connection to Dominic Serres and his family.

Ben Lacy-Hulbert has provided me with family trees and other material about the Piguenits, and Commander John Meares supplied trees linking the Burts to the Cooks, the Hatts, the Boons and the Davises. Nigel Hutchins has been very helpful in sharing information about the Boons and the Thurstons. And Arthur Leaman very kindly read what I had written about Harry and Rufus.

Sir Roger Tomkys, Master of Pembroke College, Cambridge, Dr A V Grimstone, its President, and James Campbell, an Emeritus Fellow and former Director of Studies in Law, have gone out of their ways to help me with information about Rufus' years at the College.

As far as my father's side of the family is concerned, I have learnt a lot from my grandfather's diaries and Margery's book *Young, Yesterday*. Pat Manning has greatly helped me partially untangle the early Birches, and Rafe Clutton and Eulene Moores have added considerably to my family knowledge.

My sister Elizabeth, whose memory is better than mine, has filled in many gaps in my knowledge about our parents, aunts, uncles and great-aunts.

Inevitably I have spent many hours in the Public Record Office, the Family Records Centre, the British Library, and the library of the Society of Genealogists, where the paid staff and volunteers have been invariably helpful.

I must also thank Mrs Victoria O'Flaherty of the St Kitts National Archives, Mrs Jacqueline Cramer-Armony of the St Christopher Heritage Society, and Mrs Lornette Hanley of the Nevis Historical and Conservation Society for their help when I was researching in St Kitts and Nevis. I gained much useful information from the well preserved and well looked-after records in the Department of Archives in Barbados.

I am greatly indebted to the late Canon George Walker, a former Archdeacon of St Kitts and an old family friend, for a copy of the Cayon Diary and much information about the old St Kitts families. Peter Delisle helped me with information about his family, and Professor Eric Hobsbawm kindly read what I had written about Emile Burns and suggested an addition. Arnold Rattenbury and Monty Johnstone were also helpful with information about Emile.

I am grateful to Miranda Carter, author of *Anthony Blunt: His Lives*, for generous help with information about the Cambridge Apostles, from which it seems that my uncle Rufus was not a member.

My friends in the library at Westminster Abbey -- Richard Mortimer, Keeper of the Muniments, Christine Reynolds, Assistant Keeper, and Tony Trowles, the Librarian -- have allowed me to use their Dictionary of National Biography and other reference books and provided information about the burial in the Abbey of Colonel John Davis.

I would also like to thank John Hemming, a former Director of the Royal Geographical Society, and the British Empire and Commonwealth Museum in Bristol for help when I was trying to obtain a map of St Kitts and Nevis.

To all the above, I say 'thank you very much'. To those I have not mentioned, I say, with Henry V, 'old men forget' and beg forgiveness.

CHRIS BIRCH

Fulham, July 2003

Preface

I have had my three score years and ten and am now 16 years older than my father was when he died. As old men do, I've been looking backwards at my own life and at those of my forbears.

I have been very lucky. Born and brought up in the West Indies, I left home and crossed the Atlantic at the age of 18 to go to university. There I met and married a very wonderful woman who has stayed by my side for more than half a century. And I've had an exceptionally varied and interesting life. I was an active member of the Communist Party for some 40 years. I edited an influential weekly news-magazine for more than a decade. I was living in Budapest in 1956 and witnessed the uprising at first hand. I worked at London Lighthouse in the early days of the HIV epidemic, and represented Lighthouse at Princess Diana's funeral, walking with others behind her coffin.

And I belong to the very select group of people who have put up a memorial in Westminster Abbey.

So it has not been an uneventful life. But this is not an autobiography. That may come later. It is an account, for my children and grandchildren, of what I know of some of the members of my family. They include 17th and 18th century Empire-builders, colonial governors and chief justices, immensely wealthy sugar planters, members of the British parliament, and the clergyman who conducted the secret and illegal marriage of the Prince of Wales and Mrs Fitzherbert.

Also on the family tree are Dominic Serres, marine painter to King George III, and 'Princess' Olive of Cumberland, who claimed to be the daughter of Henry Frederick, Duke of Cumberland and Strathearn, the king's brother. And, while I'm dropping names, I might as well mention Peter Townsend, who didn't marry Princess Margaret, Leonard Cheshire VC, and Hugh Gaitskell.

And one of the family married Field-Marshal Helmuth Karl Bernhardt Graf von Moltke, Chief of Staff of the Prussian Army at the time of the Austro-Prussian and Franco-Prussian wars. As if it matters! There were also the inevitable black sheep, without whom no family is complete.

I have in my computer the names and dates of some 3500 of them, and this is an attempt to add some flesh and blood to those dry bones and to put it all on paper while there is still time. I have too many unanswered questions that I should have asked my parents and grandparents before they died. I hope to leave fewer such questions for my children and grandchildren. I'll start with my father, a Victorian baby, and look slowly backwards to my forbears in the days of King Charles I.

I will also relate what I know of those old St Kitts families that are connected to mine by marriage.   CB

A story like this, by its very nature, cannot be complete
and, almost inevitably, it will contain mistakes.
The author would welcome corrections and additions.
Who knows, there might even be a revised edition
sometime in the future.

chris@sw6lon.freeserve.co.uk

Contents

Chapter 1

My father and his immediate family

*Norman goes to the West Indies, Bernard goes to Hong Kong,
and Grace, Con and Margery go off to the wars,
while their parents, who were Middle Class, Liberal
and Nonconformist, stayed at home*

You could say that my father was an unsuccessful bank clerk who drank himself to death. I did not know him very well, but that description is probably unfair. In *Young, Yesterday,* his sister Margery describes him as 'a young man of exceptional looks and charm and spirit' with 'merry blue eyes'. Some years later, in the West Indies, he acquired a reputation as a dandy and was nicknamed Gilbert after Gilbert the Filbert, the Colonel of the Knuts.

The chorus of the 1914 music hall song went like this:

I'm Gilbert, the Filbert, the Knut with a K,
The pride of Piccadilly, the blase roue.
Oh, Hades!
The ladies
Who leave their wooden huts
For Gilbert, the Filbert, the Colonel of the Knuts.

All his friends knew him as Gilbert; none of them as Norman. But it was as Norman Peyton Birch that he was ushered into the world, in Fawcett Road, Southsea, on 31 May 1890 by Dr Conan Doyle, creator of Sherlock Holmes, according to family lore. I have no proof of this but certainly Conan Doyle was an impoverished medic in Southsea at the time.

My father moved with his parents from Soutsea to Bristol and then, without his parents, from Bristol to the West Indies. This must have been quite a brave and adventurous step for a young man of 22. He had been secretary of the Bristol Young Liberals and had joined the Territorials, winning the shooting cup three times. He had a humble job in a stationer's called Baker's and then four years as a cashier with Farrow's Bank in Bristol.

Margery suggests that he may have found his Victorian and Nonconformist home somewhat cramping to his lively temper. Anyhow, he joined the Colonial Bank in January 1913 and was sent to Barbados as a clerk. His salary was £200 a year.

Between 1913 and 1916 he worked in Barbados, Demerara and Grenada before being made acting sub-manager at Mahaica, British Guiana, in 1916 and in Tobago in 1917. By 1919 he had become an acting accountant in Dominica, transferring to St Lucia in 1920 to become a full accountant.

By the end of 1920 he was back in Barbados, and by 1922 he had been again sent to Demerara. In December 1923 he transferred to St Kitts as acting accountant. And in 1925/26 the Colonial Bank and the Anglo-Egyptian Bank came together to form Barclays (Dominion, Colonial and Overseas) Bank.

The above details of my father's shuntings backwards and forwards across the Caribbean come from Barclay's archives in Manchester, which then go silent until his retirement in 1949, when it was minuted for Barclays DCO's board of directors: "N P Birch - Clerk, Barbados, retired on grounds of ill health, with a pension of £449.13.4 pa commencing 31 May 1949 at age 59, after 38 years service, which includes 2 years in respect of previous banking service - payable by the Colonial Bank Pension Fund."

I will try to fill in the gaps.

As far as I know, he stayed with the bank in St Kitts from 1923 until 1938, an amazing 15 years compared with the hithering and thithering of his first ten years in the West Indies. He was certainly in St Kitts at the time of the 1924 hurricane, as my mother remembered being told that 'poor Mr Birch' had been swept out to sea and drowned.

And he was certainly there continuously from 1927 when he got married until his transfer from St Kitts to Trinidad in 1938 apart, of course, for periods of 'long leave' in England. In 1930, when I was two, I accompanied them; in 1934, my sister and I were left with our grandparents; in 1938, the four of us crossed the Atlantic together.

I remember his sitting in a rocking chair on the verandah of our St Kitts home and bouncing me, a very small boy, on his knees as he sang

> Bumpity! Bumpity! Bumpity! Bump!
> As if I was riding my charger.
> Bumpity! Bumpity! Bumpity! Bump!
> As proud as an Indian Rajah.
> All the girls declare
> That I'm a gay old stager.
> Hey! Hey! Clear the way! Here comes the galloping major

before dropping me between his legs onto the verandah floor with a bump. I was to repeat the exercise with my own children.

My father had a Roman nose and smoked a pipe as well as Gold Flake cigarettes. He was active in the, at that time colour-barred, social life of the island. When he left, he was presented with a large elegant silver cigarette box inscribed 'Norman Peyton Birch from the members of the St Kitts Club 1933-1938'. But things were not going well at the bank.

According to my mother, the bank manager never answered letters, and Head Office as well as my father, as second-in-command, became increasingly worried. Eventually inspectors were sent out to St Kitts from Head Office, my parents entertained them to dinner, and my father was drunk. So he was transferred to Trinidad. That is what I have been told. Apparently no record has survived in the bank's archives.

My belief is that my father was a hard-working and conscientious bank accountant who could not hold his drink, and that the bank inspectors came to the wrong conclusion. Rum was, of course, very cheap in the West Indies, and there had been a longish rum-related period early in my father's time out there when he had ceased writing home to his mother. There was also a cryptic note in the Barclays staff register as follows: "Sept. 1923 - not satisfactory at Demerara. To go to St Kitts as acting accountant @ £450pa. If not well reported at St Kitts, the matter will again be considered. Mr Birch so informed."

Whether this was drink-related or not, I don't know. But he seems to have kept his copy-book clean between 1923 and 1938.

Trinidad during the war could not have been easy. It was very hot and very humid, without the redeeming sea breezes of a small island like St Kitts. There was no easily reached sea-bathing, which my father loved, although he could not swim.

And the cost of living was high. The bank manager there once remarked that it was a good thing that most of his staff had private incomes. My father did not.

The drinking continued, to the detriment of his health. Eventually, my uncle Rufus, no doubt using his Cambridge connections, pulled strings with one of the bank's directors and got my father transferred in 1945 to Barbados, where at least the sea-bathing was easily accessible. But, as already noted, he was retired on grounds of ill-health in May 1949.

Less than eight months later, he died in his mother's Bristol dining room, which had been turned into a bedroom for him. Cirrhosis of the liver. She had a horror of anyone being buried alive and had to be assured that her son really was dead and not just sleeping.

On 29 January 1950 she wrote to her niece Nesta in Teddington:

Our dear Norman passed away early yesterday (Saturday) morning, peacefully in his sleep. He had been ill so long and suffered so much that we are thankful that he is at peace. Iris has been wonderful, never complained of fatigue or want of sleep. Her great self-control has stood her in good stead. The burial will be by cremation on Wednesday but they do not wish flowers.

Iris will go on a visit to a friend in Liverpool & so get a needed change. Betty's training for Norland nursing does not begin till Apr 1st. Christopher has been here the last few days as his mother felt she needed him & he could not concentrate with his father lying between life & death. I'm afraid his studies will suffer a great deal.

My uncle Rufus arrived from Cambridge to pay his condolences. He sent a

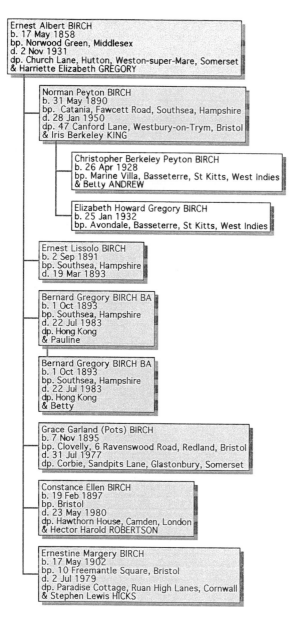

Ernest Albert BIRCH
b. 17 May 1858
bp. Norwood Green, Middlesex
d. 2 Nov 1931
dp. Church Lane, Hutton, Weston-super-Mare, Somerset
& Harriette Elizabeth GREGORY

Norman Peyton BIRCH
b. 31 May 1890
bp. Catania, Fawcett Road, Southsea, Hampshire
d. 28 Jan 1950
dp. 47 Canford Lane, Westbury-on-Trym, Bristol
& Iris Berkeley KING

Christopher Berkeley Peyton BIRCH
b. 26 Apr 1928
bp. Marine Villa, Basseterre, St Kitts, West Indies
& Betty ANDREW

Elizabeth Howard Gregory BIRCH
b. 25 Jan 1932
bp. Avondale, Basseterre, St Kitts, West Indies

Ernest Lissolo BIRCH
b. 2 Sep 1891
bp. Southsea, Hampshire
d. 19 Mar 1893

Bernard Gregory BIRCH BA
b. 1 Oct 1893
bp. Southsea, Hampshire
d. 22 Jul 1983
dp. Hong Kong
& Pauline

Bernard Gregory BIRCH BA
b. 1 Oct 1893
bp. Southsea, Hampshire
d. 22 Jul 1983
dp. Hong Kong
& Betty

Grace Garland (Pots) BIRCH
b. 7 Nov 1895
bp. Clovelly, 6 Ravenswood Road, Redland, Bristol
d. 31 Jul 1977
dp. Corbie, Sandpits Lane, Glastonbury, Somerset

Constance Ellen BIRCH
b. 19 Feb 1897
bp. Bristol
d. 23 May 1980
dp. Hawthorn House, Camden, London
& Hector Harold ROBERTSON

Ernestine Margery BIRCH
b. 17 May 1902
bp. 10 Freemantle Square, Bristol
d. 2 Jul 1979
dp. Paradise Cottage, Ruan High Lanes, Cornwall
& Stephen Lewis HICKS

cable to my West Indian grandparents saying GILBERT AT PEACE AT
LAST.

4

My father grew up in a middle-class, Liberal and Nonconformist family in Bristol. He had two brothers and three sisters. As the oldest in a Victorian family, he was undoubtedly spoiled. Margery describes how his mother would fuss over him at meals. Is it too much, too little? Would he like fewer potatoes, more gravy? "Have you got what you like, dear?". And his parents marked his 21st birthday with a garden party. None of his siblings was thus honoured.

My Hong Kong uncle

Norman's first brother was Ernest Lissolo, but he died before he was two, and he was quickly followed by Bernard Gregory who lived to be 89. My father spent his adult life in the West Indies; my Uncle Bernard spent most of his in Hong Kong. So I hardly knew him. Apart from the geographical distance that separated them, they were not close emotionally, possibly not unrelated to the fact that, when youngsters, Norman accidentally blinded Bernard in one eye while skylarking about with a pitch fork.

Margery describes Bernard as 'silent, self-absorbed, dark, sardonic'. And 'clever'. He was the only one of his siblings to go to university. In fact his name appears in the Bristol University Calendar immediately before that of Betty Birch, my wife, although more than three decades separated their graduation dates.

After graduating, Bernard went to war. On medical grounds (no doubt his blind eye), he was not accepted for active service. He was given a commission and, instead of fighting, acted as an interpreter for prisoners of war. He later taught, worked for the League of Nations in Geneva and eventually became a lecturer in the English department of the University of Hong Kong. He was there when the colony fell to the Japanese and was imprisoned. I have a letter written by him to "My dearest Mother" from Stanley Prison Camp on 19 August 1945. "Our greatest misery here was always hunger. I have been hungry every day, except perhaps six or eight, for the last three and a half years...I am also looking forward to my first bath since 1942."

He also complained of news starvation, saying that what they heard via the Japanese was 45% lies and 45% propaganda. He was later horrified to learn that the voters of Britain had rejected Churchill and elected a Labour government.

Bernard's first wife, Pauline, died in 1948. His second wife, who survived him, was called Betty.

Smiling Pots

The three boys were followed by three girls. Grace was the first of the children to be born in Bristol, after the family had moved there from Southsea. Her name was Grace Garland, but she was always known as Pots. Her father called her his Sunbeam, his Little Philosopher and his Pot of Jam. The Pot became

Pots and stuck. I got to know her and her two sisters better than I had known her brothers. My father died when I was 21, and I only met Bernard, very briefly, twice.

I remember Pots as always smiling. I expect this was the result of her faith in Christian Science. Since God is good and is Spirit, matter and evil are not real. According to Margery, she had been a serious, thoughtful child who, more than any of her siblings, had inherited her mother's nonconformist conscience with its strict regard for truth: everything for Gracie was neatly sorted into black and white, and she was deeply suspicious of intermediate shades.

She was very kind and was devoted to her mother, as were her two sisters, but she was, I think, her mother's least favourite daughter. Con and Margery were livelier and more interesting. They both got married and had more exciting lives.

Apart from the war, the first world war that is, Grace stayed at home and looked after the home. That's not to say she didn't have a job. She taught domestic science at a local girls' school, but she also did the housekeeping and most of the cooking at 47 Canford Lane and spent more time at home than any of the others. When I was living there in 1946, rhubarb frequently featured as the pudding, and I grew to loathe it.

When war broke out in 1914, Grace had just graduated from the College of Domestic Science. She turned her back on a safe job in teaching and joined the Womens' Army Auxiliary Corps. Margery remembers her arriving home on her first leave, wearing neat, form-fitting khaki.

"Never had she looked so smart. She was stationed at Rhyl in North Wales, the camp was a sea of mud, they slithered about between duckboards, were frozen with cold but ordered to wear their woolly cardigans *under* their uniform; the girls in the cookhouse sang bawdy songs -- Grace was meeting Life in the Raw."

Margery, the youngest, was the first of the girls to leave home for good -- after Norman and Bernard but before the second world war. Con did not leave home until several years after her marriage. When I arrived in Bristol from Barbados in 1946, it was to join my grandmother, Grace, Connie and Robbie in the small house in Westbury-on-Trym. It was quite a tight squeeze.

I soon found a place in a university hall of residence, and Con and Rob found a home of their own. But Grace stayed on to be rejoined later by Margery, when she was doing teacher-training in Bristol.

Grace only twice ventured abroad, and both trips were disastrous. She went on a package holiday to Spain but found the heat unbearable and took the next plane home.

Then, some years later, she flew to Hong Kong to visit her brother and found herself out of her depth socially. It seems that, when entertained by some of Bernard's friends, she failed to offer her hosts a gift. Bernard was furious and wanted nothing more to do with her. Poor, unsophisticated, naive Grace flew home in disgrace. Her sisters found it hard to forgive their brother.

After her mother died in 1952, Grace left Canford Lane and lived alone in Bristol but she spent her last weeks at Con's home in Glastonbury, where my sister helped to care for her. She died there in 1977, aged 81.

Bouncy Connie

Constance Ellen, born in 1897, was as bouncy and extrovert as Grace was quiet and meditative. Ebullient and gregarious, she was an organiser, a leader, the cream that rises naturally to the surface. Cheerful and confident, it was natural for her to become prefect, captain of games, and head girl of the school, liked by staff and idolised by the younger girls.

When I first got to know her, during the six months I spent in England in 1938, she was secretary to Bristol's Chief Education Officer. By the time I returned to Bristol eight years later, she had become the first head of Bristol's Nursery Schools Department, or was it the Primary Schools Department? She was first one and then the other.

During the war, she drove an ambulance in Bristol, and in 1944 she surprised most of us by marrying the lodger.

Robbie was a brewer and had been married before. He and Con met at the tennis club, and it seems to have been a very happy marriage. Always smiling, always kind, they both exuded happiness. They lived together at Long Ashton, just outside Bristol; in Newport, Monmouthshire; Shepton Mallet and then Butleigh in Somerset; and finally Glastonbury, the name of their house, 'Corbie', moving with them.

Connie, like Grace, was a life-long Christian Scientist and died in a Christian Science hospice in London in 1980, aged 83. She had lived longer than both her sisters.

Margery, my favourite aunt

Margery was my favourite aunt. She wasn't a Christian Scientist, she drank, she was artistic and she seemed more fun. When I fell in love with another undergraduate called Ruth, it was to Margery that I turned for advice. Margery's pensive portrait in oils hangs on my living-room wall, alongside the unsmiling portrait of her mother, by the same artist, Allan Davidson. He exhibited frequently at the Royal Academy and lived at Walberswick in Suffolk, and I think that Margery must have got to know him when she was weaving at Safron Walden.

Her father's leather-bound diary for 1902 records laconically: "Ernestine Margery born on my birthday May 17th Saturday at 8.38 in the evening". The births of Norman, Bernard, Grace and Con had occasioned paragraphs of delight and pride. But for Margery there was no accolade, no joyful thanksgiving. By then her father had had enough. Indeed, two pages later his diary comes to an abrupt end.

At Colston Girls School in Bristol (motto: 'Go and do thou likewise'), where both her sisters had been, Margery won a prize for art work in 1918 and a prize for English the following year. When she left school, she went to the College of Art and then worked for several years as a handweaver with the Snows at Trout Hall, Wendens Ambo, Safron Walden in Essex.

She was a friend of Judith Masefield, the Poet Laureate's daughter, and I have two handwritten letters from him to Margery, both signed John Masefield, one thanking her for "the kind gift of the tie, so generously woven for me". According to Margery, Judith was somewhat absent minded. When clearing up after a meal at the Masefields' Abingdon home, with Margery washing up and Judith drying, Judith would carefully dry a plate and then, equally carefully, replace it in the sink with the dirty dishes.

Margery's war diaries are now in the Department of Documents at the Imperial War Museum. After hearing Chamberlain's broadcast on Sunday 3 September 1939, she and her friend Patience "spent Monday & Tuesday, the 4th and 5th, phoning places trying to join up. On Wednesday, after reading an article in the *Telegraph*, we went to Chigwell & joined the W.A.A.Fs".

By January 1940 she was a corporal, and by August that year she was Assistant Section Officer Birch and working as a cypher officer.

Her journal for 6 June 1944, D Day, describes the long-awaited invasion of France. "At 0130 hours I climbed on the ops roof to see the most amazing sight I've ever seen: on the runway our fleet of tugs and gliders were taking off perfectly timed; above them at about 5000ft came a great formation of US Dakotas flying in V formation of 3 in a flight -- the sky was full of twinkly green and red and amber lights, the air filled with the steady, purposeful roar of their engines.

"Away in the distance came another fleet, and further off still a haze of lights betokened still another. Our aircraft and tows circled below them before streaming off to the south. And as they went, the first bombers came back ...."

She was, I believe, the first woman to be made an adjutant in the air force.

After the war, she joined her friends the Grinlingtons on St Agnes in the Isles of Scilly and worked as a flower farmer for three and a half years, from 1945 to 1948. I spent the whole of my first summer vacation in England, in 1947, working with her on 'her' flower farm. I say 'her' but the farm probably belonged to the Duchy of Cornwall, and Mrs Grinlington (Colonel Grinlington had died), Wendy and Archie Aldridge, and Margery were tenants. She then did a teacher training course in Bristol and taught for a while until 1952, when she married another flower farmer from St Agnes, Stephen Lewis Hicks. She was 50; he was 69.

After retiring from flower farming in 1955, they settled in Cornwall, buying a little house called Paradise Cottage, where Margery wove and wrote. *Young, Yesterday*, an account of her childhood set mainly in Bristol, was published in 1969. *The Happy Year*, a novel about flower farming in the Scilly Isles, followed eight years later.

When Margery married Stephen Lewis, 19 years her senior, she never imagined that he would outlive her, but he did. She died on 2 July 1979, aged 77. Her heart-broken husband died eight weeks later.

Ernest and Elizabeth, my Birch grandparents

I first met my Birch grandparents when I stayed with them in their cottage at Hutton near Weston-super-Mare in Somerset, but I was only two so I remember nothing of that visit. When I paid my second visit to England in 1938, my grandfather had been dead for more than six years. My knowledge of him is derived from his diaries and from Margery's first book. The first sentence of *Young, Yesterday* was 'Our family was Middle Class, Liberal and Nonconformist and this -- so I understood -- was a Most Desirable Thing'.

The diaries give an amazingly detailed picture of his life in the final quarter of the 19th century but, although his copperplate handwriting is easily readable most of the time, there are numerous words and abbreviations that defeat me. It is clear, however, that he was a deeply religious man, fanatically so it may seem to a 21st century reader.

Sundays were a long round of Sunday school, morning service, an orange for lunch, afternoon service, evening service, distribution of temperance tracts, and bible studies. He often preached himself and played the harmonium. "Had a blessed time" is a frequently recurring phrase. And he travelled about spreading the word of the Lord. I have a leaflet printed by the Wesleyan Sunday School in Stalbridge, Dorset, announcing that on Sunday, June 26, 1887, sermons will be preached by Mr E Birch of Southsea at 11am and at 6.30pm.

He was equally busy and hardworking in the family grocery business, first at Ealing, later at Southsea. We learn from his diary that on 23 August 1884 he "Rose at 5.30. Fred & I began on orders, & we counted our customers by putting peas in a tin & in 2 hours from 7am to 9 we had 54 customers. Were regularly busy all day. Edw drove Eastncy round. I was nearly knocked up at night what with the oppressive heat & being so busy."

And the same day saw a major excitement. "Edw & Bessie [his elder brother and his wife] took a boat from the beach & rowed to the Victory. In returning they got into the dangerous parts & nearly paid for it with their lives. The boatman said had they capsized nothing could have saved them. B. said she never prayed so earnestly in her life. They thought their hour had come."

But my grandfather was not happy as a grocer. On 31 January 1884 he wrote: "The past 3 days have been very poor ones. I feel sometimes has (sic) if I cannot be a grocer & when I think of my plans etc all smashed, I could cry &

a good deal more. Others in similar spheres & lower serve God and are content; I feel as if I am living below what I ought to be, yet do not see my way clear out of it or any opening for a nobler life."

Six months later, after 11 years as a grocer, the opening appeared, and he became a travelling insurance agent for the General Life & Fire Office. It seems that his two jobs continued in parallel for some time, but by the time he moved his family to Bristol in 1894 it was to become branch manager of the General Life Assurance Company.

Like my King grandfather, my Birch grandfather was a prolific writer. His diaries, filling several large volumes, were handwritten but, after he acquired a secondhand Smith Premier typewriter, the letters, poems and religious tracts poured forth. I have a few of the printed pamphlets that have survived. *Lady Helen's Carriage* is unpriced but *The Clock Shop* and the prophetic *The Royal Show in the Year Two Thousand* sold for twopence and *Three Stories High* for threepence. They appeared before the first world war.

Through Many Windows - Some Modern Parables (1914) and *Margery's Shop* (1919) were proper hardback books with a Fleet Street publisher, and the latter had his daughter's photograph as frontispiece.

His diary records the beginning of my grandparents' courtship. "*Jan 4th 1888. I walked back from watch night service with Miss Gregory.*" And later: "On May 7th 1889 at 2pm, being twelve months and thirty three days after my first proposing, we were married at Elm Grove Baptist Chapel ..."

It seems to have been an exceptionally happy marriage. His letters to his wife begin 'Dearest One'. In a letter to Cyril Moores written in 1924, he says "I am keeping up a honey-moon of nearly thirty-five years, & it is a jolly sight better at this end than it was at the other end, the beginning". In his last Will and Testament, he gives all his property "to my dear Wife Harriette Elizabeth Birch only regretting that I can leave her so little and so much less than she deserves she having been the perfection of wives and the very best of mothers to our dear children".

He died on 2 November 1931 at Hutton, Weston-super-Mare, leaving a gross estate of £539 14s 7d.

Harriette Elizabeth Gregory was a formidable lady. Born on 8 October 1863 in West Leamington, the fourth child of George Peyton Gregory, a cabinet-maker, she lived to be 88. Neither my wife nor my sister liked her, and they both say that she disliked them. When my West Indian grandparents visited her in the 1930s, it was my grandfather to whom she talked, ignoring his wife. But I was a man, and that made a lot of difference to her.

I saw quite a lot of her between my arrival in Bristol in 1946 and my moving to London in 1951, and we got on reasonably well. She had had an incendiary bomb in her kitchen during the war, and there was still an Anderson air-raid shelter in her garden when I stayed with her during my first university term.

As I remember her, she was exactly like her Allan Davidson portrait, which must have been painted more than a decade earlier as he died in 1932. She seemed to be wearing the same outfit, or one very similar: a dull blue loose-fitting cardigan and scarf, as she sat by her living-room fire, reading, with her dictionary, atlas and wireless, as she called it, close at hand. Her wireless was permanently tuned to the BBC's Home Service, and she did not like anyone to fiddle with it. In those days there was also the Light Programme and the Third Programme, but she was afraid that, if the wave length was changed, she might never find her way back to the Home Service again.

Her spinning-wheel, which she still occasionally used in the late 1940s, stood in the corner.

She was a great reader and greatly interested in spiritual matters, being at different times Baptist, Christian Scientist and Buddhist, picking and mixing from the world's religions and philosophies as she went through life. She was cosseted by her daughters, and a few months before her death wrote in *House-wife* "I am still enjoying life thoroughly, with no responsibilities or worries, the luxury of occasional car rides, plenty of time for reading, spinning and writing. So at 87 I feel I have reached a peak of happiness, and life is very, very good."

Margery wrote to us in January 1952 to say that her mother's life was drawing to its close. I hope I wrote to say good-bye. I am ashamed that I did not take time off from work to visit her or attend her funeral.

Chapter 2

Earlier Birches, Garlands and asssorted cousins

Five Birches called John, Lord Howe's steward,
Garibaldi's friend , the beautiful and talented Rica,
and the mystery of the Waterloo Box

We now come to two Johns, father and son, both grocers. My grandfather's father, John Birch (1832-1914), was the son of John Birch (1801-1889), known as 'Big Large', a grocer in Amersham High Street, Buckinghamshire, and his wife Alice Rogers (1802-1853). John the younger left home in Amersham before the 1851 census to run a bakery and grocery business in Norwood Green, West London. In 1853 he married Ellen Garland.

At the time of the 1861 census he had three employees living with him, and it seems that in 1863 he built, or started building, 17 cottages in Norwood Terrace. In the wall opposite the cottages there is to this day a stone that says simply: J BIRCH 1863. By that time he was also the postmaster.

Genealogical research has been complicated by the fact that there was another John Birch (1836-1897), probably related, who was also a baker and post-master in Norwood Green. This John, who was also a corn dealer, became postmaster in the 1890s, while my great-grandfather had been postmaster in 1863, before handing over the post office to a James Harris.

It has been pointed out by a fellow genealogist, Pat Manning, that the great-grandfather of this second John Birch (1836-1897), Robert Birch (1738-1809), had a brother John, who was born in 1736, and that a John Birch, who might have been this brother, had an illegitimate child also called John by Elizabeth Barnes, who might have been the sister of Robert's wife, Catherine.

Are you still with me? If not, never mind! Anyhow, this illegitimate child called John could have been the father of John Birch, the Amersham grocer, and the grandfather of John Birch, the baker, grocer and postmaster of Norwood Green. Be that as it may, by 1881 my great-grandfather was farming 32 acres at White Thorn House, Stoke Mandeville, Buckinghamshire, while continuing to own his grocery and bakery businesses in Norwood Green and Ealing, where my grandfather, and his brother Edward, worked.

I don't know how long the farm remained in the family but in October 1883 John Birch bought businesses in Southsea and Eastney, and the *Bucks Herald* and the *Aylesbury Advertiser* for 28 November 1883 carried notices for the sale of Whitethorn.

My great-grandfather's close-set eyes stare at me out of a humourless unsmiling face adorned with a neat white beard and resting on a high collar.

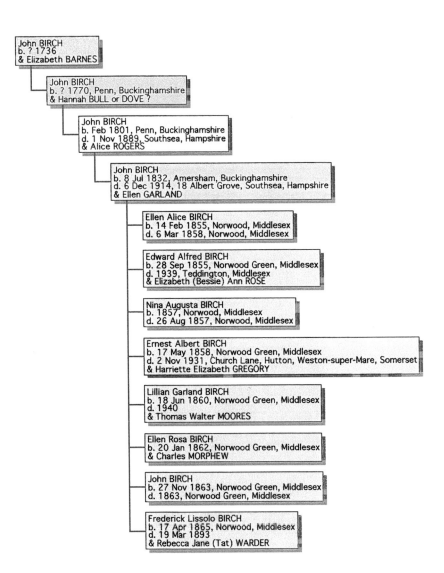

John BIRCH
b. ? 1736
& Elizabeth BARNES

John BIRCH
b. ? 1770, Penn, Buckinghamshire
& Hannah BULL or DOVE ?

John BIRCH
b. Feb 1801, Penn, Buckinghamshire
d. 1 Nov 1889, Southsea, Hampshire
& Alice ROGERS

John BIRCH
b. 8 Jul 1832, Amersham, Buckinghamshire
d. 6 Dec 1914, 18 Albert Grove, Southsea, Hampshire
& Ellen GARLAND

Ellen Alice BIRCH
b. 14 Feb 1855, Norwood, Middlesex
d. 6 Mar 1858, Norwood, Middlesex

Edward Alfred BIRCH
b. 28 Sep 1855, Norwood Green, Middlesex
d. 1939, Teddington, Middlesex
& Elizabeth (Bessie) Ann ROSE

Nina Augusta BIRCH
b. 1857, Norwood, Middlesex
d. 26 Aug 1857, Norwood, Middlesex

Ernest Albert BIRCH
b. 17 May 1858, Norwood Green, Middlesex
d. 2 Nov 1931, Church Lane, Hutton, Weston-super-Mare, Somerset
& Harriette Elizabeth GREGORY

Lillian Garland BIRCH
b. 18 Jun 1860, Norwood Green, Middlesex
d. 1940
& Thomas Walter MOORES

Ellen Rosa BIRCH
b. 20 Jan 1862, Norwood Green, Middlesex
& Charles MORPHEW

John BIRCH
b. 27 Nov 1863, Norwood Green, Middlesex
d. 1863, Norwood Green, Middlesex

Frederick Lissolo BIRCH
b. 17 Apr 1865, Norwood, Middlesex
d. 19 Mar 1893
& Rebecca Jane (Tat) WARDER

He was probably the most affluent of the Birches. Bernard certainly thought so.
I am not surprised that his daughter-in-law "never *really* cared for him",
according to Margery, and that Margery herself disliked him.

He died at 18 Albert Grove, Southsea, on 6 December 1914, leaving an
estate worth £4,370 2s 2d.

The Garlands

About the earlier Birches I know little except for a few names and dates. As already mentioned, my great-great-grandfather John Birch was a grocer in Amersham, and both his father and his grandfather were also called John. But I know a little about the Garlands, and some of it is interesting.

As you know, my great-grandmother was Ellen Garland; she had married John Birch no 4 in 1853 in the Church of the Holy Trinity, Penn. Her father was Charles Garland (1784-1846), and he was a carpenter who was employed first as estate builder and later as steward by Lord Howe on his estate at Penn.

Charles converted to Methodism from the Church of England after his wife had heard a sermon preached by Dr Adam Clarke, and the story is that Lord Howe's steward sacked him from his job on the estate after telling him to give up Methodism or be dismissed. But on his return to Penn three years later, Lord Howe sacked the steward and gave the job to Garland. This story, somewhat embellished, appeared in *The Methodist* for 13 August 1936.

Ellen lived to be 88, dying in 1911 three years before her husband. She left behind two remarkable documents. Towards the end of her life, she wrote a 75-verse poem, describing in morbid detail her family history for her granddaughter Rica. A few verses will give its flavour.

> The first was little Charles, dear,
> It was the Sabbath day;
> He chanced too near the fire
> While happy at his play.
>
> A scream -- then to the Chapel
> Where Mother was, you know.
> The place was near, so Mary
> Had not so far to go.
>
> Our little burned brother
> Lingered from day to day,
> But he at last passed from us,
> He had not long to stay.
>
> My eldest sister, Mary,
> Lingered in a decline,
> And passed away to Heaven
> Ere she was twenty-nine.

And so it goes on. Elizabeth dies. Phillip dies. So does her dear brother John. She had ten siblings, and only half of them survived beyond the age of 28.

I do not know when she wrote that poem but in 1906 she wrote a remarkable

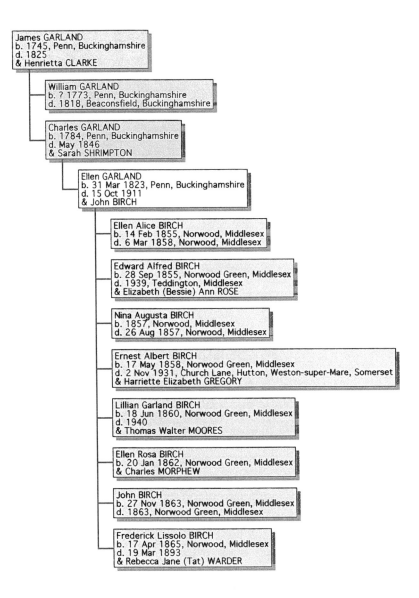

James GARLAND
b. 1745, Penn, Buckinghamshire
d. 1825
& Henrietta CLARKE

William GARLAND
b. ? 1773, Penn, Buckinghamshire
d. 1818, Beaconsfield, Buckinghamshire

Charles GARLAND
b. 1784, Penn, Buckinghamshire
d. May 1846
& Sarah SHRIMPTON

Ellen GARLAND
b. 31 Mar 1823, Penn, Buckinghamshire
d. 15 Oct 1911
& John BIRCH

Ellen Alice BIRCH
b. 14 Feb 1855, Norwood, Middlesex
d. 6 Mar 1858, Norwood, Middlesex

Edward Alfred BIRCH
b. 28 Sep 1855, Norwood Green, Middlesex
d. 1939, Teddington, Middlesex
& Elizabeth (Bessie) Ann ROSE

Nina Augusta BIRCH
b. 1857, Norwood, Middlesex
d. 26 Aug 1857, Norwood, Middlesex

Ernest Albert BIRCH
b. 17 May 1858, Norwood Green, Middlesex
d. 2 Nov 1931, Church Lane, Hutton, Weston-super-Mare, Somerset
& Harriette Elizabeth GREGORY

Lillian Garland BIRCH
b. 18 Jun 1860, Norwood Green, Middlesex
d. 1940
& Thomas Walter MOORES

Ellen Rosa BIRCH
b. 20 Jan 1862, Norwood Green, Middlesex
& Charles MORPHEW

John BIRCH
b. 27 Nov 1863, Norwood Green, Middlesex
d. 1863, Norwood Green, Middlesex

Frederick Lissolo BIRCH
b. 17 Apr 1865, Norwood, Middlesex
d. 19 Mar 1893
& Rebecca Jane (Tat) WARDER

Christmas letter to her daughter Lillian Moores, "telling some incidents in my long life". It seems that Lillian's husband Walter and her two eldest sons were in Canada and that Lillian was soon to join them.

Ellen describes her childhood in Penn, during the reign of George IV, who, she says, "died through gluttony and drunkenness". "We went to bed early; there was no light but a rush light; and we rose early, especially when it was the day for the poor sweep boys to go up the chimney, to see his broom come out at the top .... Someone had to strike with flint and steel to get a light, and put a brimstone match to it to get light, for there were no lucifcer matches until 1834. There was no gas then, so the service in the church was held in the afternoon."

"We had but few letters; there was no Post Office in the village but an old woman named Betty Channer went to Beaconsfield, two and a half miles, all weathers, every morning except Sunday, to fetch them; the postage was 6d and 2d for herself; there were no envelopes; the letters had to be folded so, so, and sealed with wax. What joy there was in 1840 when the 1d post was announced, and then in 1861 the ha'penny postcard."

Ellen lived in five reigns: George IV, William IV, Victoria, Edward VII and George V. During Ellen's childhood, William IV twice came to the village to visit Earl Howe, and she and her parents were invited to the vicarage grounds to see the king and Queen Adelaide.

In her letter Ellen describes being taken to Windsor by her father in 1841 soon after the Prince of Wales was born. "We saw the Queen and the Prince Consort come on to the terrace, and a nurse with the young prince in her arms, the band playing, the flowers blooming all so bright. Ah, me! Poor Queen. She looked happy then, but she had many sorrows in after years."

But it was not all sorrow. "There was great rejoicing in 1863, when the Prince of Wales was married. All the children in the parish of Southall had tea on Norwood Green. Four bakers had to make the cake for them, and ours was said by all to be the best. How many things happened for good during Victoria's long reign.... Window tax abolished 1857. Slavery no longer in United States 1857. Chloroform found out and used in 1837. Post Office Savings Bank in 1861. Bank Holiday in 1868. Drinking fountains in London in 1859. There were no telegrams till 1857, no electric trams till 1883, no telephones till 1876."

Some of these dates are not quite right but 'many things happened for good' during Ellen's lifetime.

She continues: "I saw the dear Queen at Osborne not long before she died. She was in a small low carriage, with one outrider. She had on a shabby looking old hat that many of her servants would not have worn. She died in 1901. I saw her body borne along in the boat from Osborne, to be taken to Windsor. Then King Edward began his reign ....I saw him a few days after he was King."

Ellen visited Paris twice and travelled to Milan, Venice and Verona. She nearly lost her life in Italy in 1872 in a flood, escaping over the roof of the house at night and being "led over a plank by a big Italian holding my hands and he walking backward to a safe place". The only two photographs I have of her show a grim-faced bonneted old lady with bird-like eyes and nose. It is difficult to imagine her walking the plank with a big Italian.

Great Uncle Edward
John and Ellen Birch's first-born, Ellen Alice, died when she was just three after a fall, due, according to my grandfather's diary, to "a servant's carelessness". But their next child, Edward Alfred, lived to be 83, dying in 1939. He lived in a large house at 118 Stanley Road, Teddington, and I visited him there when I was in England in 1938.

His granddaughter, Gwenneth Bradley, was still living there, with a variety of lodgers, when she died in 2002, aged 84. Her father, William Edwin Garman, had been a Methodist missionary, and she was born in India, in Hyderabad.

Edward married Elizabeth (Bessie) Ann Rose, and their first child was Nesta. She was tall and thin and musical. In fact she was a composer, although her only published composition was *The Milkmaid's Delight*, copyright, 1918, by the Anglo-French Music Co Ltd. I have a copy of it, obtained from the British Library.

I have some snaps of Nesta at the Regent's Park Zoo in 1938 together with my sister and me, our mother, our King grandmother and Con, all of us wearing hats!

Edward's and Bessie's fourth child, Wilberforce, was, according to Margery, one of the family's blackish sheep. He refused to join his father in the insurance agency business that Edward conducted from his Teddington home because he wanted to go to Canada to join the Royal Canadian Mounted Police, which he did at quite an early age. Unfortunately, he contracted tuberculosis which put an end to his police career. He returned to England, as his son Trevor was born in Teddington in 1921, but Wilbur died in Canada in 1941.

Trevor, and Trevor's children, Gary and Dorinda, live in British Columbia. Gary is the only Canadian Birch I have met. He is a marine biologist and has two sons, Daniel and Patrick. They should carry the Birch surname well into the 21st century.

Edward's and Bessie's seventh child was Rosalie. She married Robin Clutton, and I am in touch with two of their children, my second cousins, Iris Brewer and Rafe Clutton. Iris, who later became a psychiatric nurse, had an adventurous escape by yacht from nazi Germany just before the start of the second world war. Rafe became a distinguished chartered surveyor and was appointed CBE.

He too is interested in genealogy and can trace his ancestors back eleven generations to Owen Clutton in the 16th century. Rafe's grandfather, John Henry Clutton, was three times mayor of Ramsgate. He was, it seems, an awful snob and disapproved of his son (Rafe's father) Robin's marriage to Rosalie Birch and refused to attend their wedding. But his wife did go!

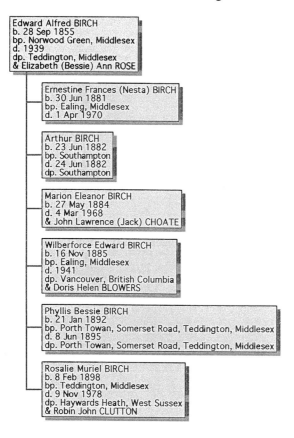

Edward Alfred BIRCH
b. 28 Sep 1855
bp. Norwood Green, Middlesex
d. 1939
dp. Teddington, Middlesex
& Elizabeth (Bessie) Ann ROSE

Ernestine Frances (Nesta) BIRCH
b. 30 Jun 1881
bp. Ealing, Middlesex
d. 1 Apr 1970

Arthur BIRCH
b. 23 Jun 1882
bp. Southampton
d. 24 Jun 1882
dp. Southampton

Marion Eleanor BIRCH
b. 27 May 1884
d. 4 Mar 1968
& John Lawrence (Jack) CHOATE

Wilberforce Edward BIRCH
b. 16 Nov 1885
bp. Ealing, Middlesex
d. 1941
dp. Vancouver, British Columbia
& Doris Helen BLOWERS

Phyllis Bessie BIRCH
b. 21 Jan 1892
bp. Porth Towan, Somerset Road, Teddington, Middlesex
d. 8 Jun 1895
dp. Porth Towan, Somerset Road, Teddington, Middlesex

Rosalie Muriel BIRCH
b. 8 Feb 1898
bp. Teddington, Middlesex
d. 9 Nov 1978
dp. Haywards Heath, West Sussex
& Robin John CLUTTON

The Canadian Birches whom I haven't met are the descendants of Lilian Garland Birch and Thomas Walter Moores. My grandfather describes in his diary how Walter was late for his own wedding.

Monday Oct 28 1884. Lilly's Wedding Day. I rose at 6.15. Prayer & then to books. Lilly awoke with a headache. I read part Psalm 35 & led prayers, praying especially for Walter & L. Also for Bessie who is very bad, in bed for a week. Mr Moores Senr & Miss M arrived by early train. Mr M, Rose, Mother & I went in the 1st carriage to Elm Grove at 11 Punctual. Finding Walter had not arvd, I started for him & before we could get back, the other carg containg Miss M, the Bride & Father arrived, so W and I were last.

Walter and Lilly had eight children. Their first child, Mabel, married Henry James Harris. They were the parents of Walter Harris, and I will describe in a moment how I met him. Walter's and Lilly's seventh child, Cyril, was the father of David Moores, whose wife Eulene shares my interest in family history. It is largely through her that I know what I know of Lilly's descendants in Canada.

But back to Walter Harris. In April 1997, my wife Betty and I were on our way to Bristol and decided to call on Walter, then living in Reading. We had corresponded for three years but had never met. He warmly welcomed us, gave us coffee, and showed us two silver tablespoons, each apparently inscribed SSG to JEB, although it is difficult to read the initials with certainty. He seemed to think that the JEB referred to John Birch, but I have no evidence of a middle name beginning with E or anything else.

However, just as we were leaving, we noticed on the wall a painting of a forest scene bearing a marked resemblance to one hanging in our own home. Closer examination proved it to be the same scene by the same artist, Betty's aunt, Irene Cullis. And it turned out that Walter knew her well, as he had been for many years Baptist minister in Coleford, in the Forest of Dean, where Rene lives. A totally unexpected connection between Betty's family and mine. Quite a coincidence!

My second cousins

Walter Harris died in 2000. He was my second cousin, as are Trevor Birch in Canada; Gwenneth Bradley, who lived at her grandfather's house in Teddington until her death in July 2002; Iris Brewer and Rafe Clutton, both living in East Sussex; and David Moores also in Canada, but in Alberta, not British Columbia.

Iris and Rafe have a younger brother Nigel, whom I have not met, who lives at Arundel with his third wife, the daughter of the man who organised the last two coronations, the 16th Duke of Norfolk. And they have a sister Marigold, who lives with a widower at Hurstpierpoint, while her husband lives with an old girlfriend in Brighton.

Another second cousin, whom I knew quite well, was Miriam Emms. My sister Betty knew her much better than I did. Miriam stayed with Betty in the Lake District every year; they were Con's joint executors; and Betty helped to look after Miriam when she became ill. She died in 1993.

Miriam's grandfather was Frederick Lissolo Birch, the eighth and youngest child of John and Ellen Birch. In 1891 Fred married Rebecca Jane Warder, known, I don't know why, as Auntie Tat. Their daughter Frederika was born on 19 February 1893. A month later, 19 March, Fred was dead. According to Margery, Fred's young widow was as pretty and penniless as any heroine in romantic fiction when she brought her baby to live with her in-laws at Southsea. Every summer Rica and Auntie Tat spent their holidays in Bristol with my grandparents. Baby Rica grew up to be as pretty as her mother. She was

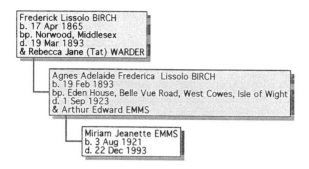

Frederick Lissolo BIRCH
b. 17 Apr 1865
bp. Norwood, Middlesex
d. 19 Mar 1893
& Rebecca Jane (Tat) WARDER

Agnes Adelaide Frederica Lissolo BIRCH
b. 19 Feb 1893
bp. Eden House, Belle Vue Road, West Cowes, Isle of Wight
d. 1 Sep 1923
& Arthur Edward EMMS

Miriam Jeanette EMMS
b. 3 Aug 1921
d. 22 Dec 1993

also delicate and musically talented. My grandfather, who adored pretty women, bought a second-hand Chappell concert grand for her. She could not eat eggs or ice-cream. She could not play cricket or rounders or help with the washing-up or weed the garden or do anything that might stiffen the joints or hurt the hands that were insured for £2000.

Soon she was giving a recitals at the Victoria Rooms. Then she became ill and had to go into a TB sanatorium. It was there that she met a good-looking violinist, Arthur Emms. Against the advice of their consultant, they got married, and Miriam was born a year later, in August 1921. Then Arthur died, on 26 January 1922.

Miriam was five months old.

Rica went on working at the piano. She taught and gave more recitals. She played with the Bournemouth Symphony under Dan Godfrey -- not yet Sir Dan. She had an audition with Sir Henry Wood who engaged her to play at a Promenade Concert. Then, quite suddenly, she died, aged 30. Miriam was two and an orphan.

At first her grandmother, Auntie Tat, looked after her. But Auntie Tat then became ill and had to go into hospital, and a wealthy admirer of Rica's, who had often driven her to and from her concerts, welcomed Miriam into his home. Like a fairy godmother, Ben Veysey took her to the large department store in Bournemouth that he owned and had her kitted out with everything she needed.

Miriam was 13 when her grandmother died. As she grew up, it became clear that, like her parents, Miriam was exceptionally musical. And it seems that contact with her father's family was lost. In fact Miriam came to believe that they had washed their hands of her.

Consequently she greatly valued her relationships with the surviving members of her mother's family, frequently visiting and staying with the

Birches at Canford Lane and with Margery, Con and my sister in their own homes.

She studied the piano under Cyril Smith at the Royal College of Music and graduated with both music and teaching qualifications. Her first appointment, at a large school in a deprived area in the North East, was such a traumatic experience that she had a breakdown. After psychiatric treatment, she joined the staff of the Hall School in Wincanton but had to go into hospital again. Her doctor suggested that she should take up smoking in order to steady her nerves. She lived to be 72 but lung cancer got her in the end.

Her mental breakdown made Miriam specially sensitive to to the needs of the mentally ill, and at the Hall School she encouraged the older girls to help at a weekly social club for mentally handicapped young adults.

She took early retirement after 34 years at the school, during which time she had acted as Head and had initiated two other Head Mistresses. She then return-ed to the home in Alton of her benefactor's widow, Marie Veysey. There she dedicated her life to work for the Religious Society of Friends, the Quakers, serving as monthly meeting clerk for six years. For ten years she was secretary of the Alton Council of Churches.

About four years before she died, something wonderful happened. Miriam's landlady saw in the *News of the World* an advertisement inserted by the executor of Miriam's father's sister, Violet Emms, seeking news of Miriam! She replied and was surprised and gratified to discover that she had been cherished as a baby and little girl by her aunt and by her father's mother and that her grandfather Emms had left her money in trust until she was 21. Sadly, by now, all three were dead, but Miriam was to meet the daughter of her father's eldest step-brother, then 90 years old, and *her* daughter Shirley.

I must add a postscript. In 1970 Margery received an amazing letter from a Stanley E Collingwood. His second wife, a Bristolian, had read *Young, Yesterday*, but he had not been the least bit interested. Bored, in fact. Until he realised that the Rica in the book was the Rica he had known in Southsea in 1919. It was he who had driven her to her audition with Sir Henry Wood. He had taken her to the Midhurst Sanatorium and had visited her there regularly, getting to know Arthur Emms as well. He used to take her to lessons with Tobias Matthay, who was also teaching Myra Hess and Moiseiwitsch.

Mr Collingwood told Margery "My son still plays the lovely *rondo* Arthur composed and laid on Rica's plate one birthday morning". His letter ends: "I am now in my 82nd year but can recall so vividly all that transpired during our all too short a time with the lovely, gracious, beautiful Rica Birch. She *was* a genius and her death at so young an age was a tragic loss to the whole musical world".

Two more second cousins, who are only names to me, are Phyllis and Joan Morphew. Did they marry? Are they still alive? I wish I knew. Their father,

Reggie Morphew, was brought up in Bristol by my Birch grandparents. Wilbur Birch, Edward's son, may have been a blackish sheep. Reggie's father Charlie was definitely a black sheep. He drank.

John and Ellen Birch's sixth child Rose had married Charlie Morphew, and they had five sons. How long Charlie had been drinking and with what consequences, I don't know, but at some stage his father-in-law decided that enough was enough and called a family conference. John Birch and his two sons, Edward and Ernest, descended on the Morphew home. Young Reggie was dispatched to my grandmother in Bristol, without a word of warning, and Reggie's younger brother Harold was dumped on his Auntie Bessie in Teddington.

When my great-grandmother came to stay in Bristol, she lectured Reggie on his good fortune, reminding him that, if it weren't for my grandfather's charity, he would be in a Home. Harold must have found his lot with Uncle Edward even more bitter: he ran away. Rose was left in a house in Norwood Green belonging to her father and, in return, collected his rents for him.

History does not relate what was done with Charlie and his other three sons, two of whom died young, but it seems that Charlie died in South Africa.

The mystery of the Waterloo Box

Before leaving my father's paternal ancestors and turning to Granny Birch's family, I must tell you about the Waterloo Box. I inherited from my father an oaken box with a sliding lid and lock. The key and a little metal key-ring have survived, and the lock still works. Inside the box was a single sheet of ruled yellowing paper with the following handwritten message:

> This Box was a work Box used by Captain William Garland. He was a Captain in a Regiment of Horse Soldiers Hussars, I forget the number. He was in the battle of Waterloo, he had been in nine engagements but never was injured, although once His Horse was shot under Him. He retired after the battle of Waterloo and lived in a large Gothic House in High Street Beaconsfield Bucks. I remember as a girl at home having some part of his Regimentals Especially a scarf. I kept that for years and once made a purse out of a piece of it and gave to Ernest. Don't know if he as (sic) it still. He was a very Proud man and kept aloof from his Mother and Brothers, he was not married. He had a man Servant and his wife who was the house keeper. He was taken ill and died. The man and his wife robbed him of money and valuables and started to America, there was a Great Storm the vessel sank and they went down in it ---- All this and more that I forget as (sic) been told me by My Mother years ago I had forgotten till I see this box again after Aunt Lissolo death. She had it with her in all her travels in Italy ---- I leave this for any one who as (sic) the Box when we are gone ----
>
> Feb 21st 1909   Ellen Garland

The above was no doubt written by my great-grandmother, Ellen Birch. The

Ernest to whom she gave the purse made from Capt Garland's scarf was my grandfather, and Aunt Lissolo would have been Ellen's sister Sarah Garland, who married the Revd Benditto Lissolo. He must have been an interesting man. He was 'the first Roman Catholic priest in Wesleyan Methodism in Italy', whatever that means, and a friend of Garibaldi.

I imagine that Ellen called her sister Aunt because her children called her that, and Aunt Lissolo instead of Aunt Sarah because there was already an Aunt Sarah, the wife of Ellen's brother John. But it is a little strange that my great-grandmother should have signed her note about the box Ellen Garland and not Ellen Birch. Perhaps she wanted to emphasise her connection with the box's owner, William Garland. If so, it is a pity she didn't say exactly what her relationship to him was.

It is even stranger that the signature 'Ellen Garland' at the end of the note is quite different from the 'Ellen Garland' in the family bible now in the possession of my daughter Harriet. The bible had belonged to an Elizabeth Garland, probably Ellen'sister, and Ellen's marriage is recorded on the flyleaf:

Ellen Garland
Born March 31st, 1823
Married to John Birch February 26th, 1853 in
Penn Church, Buckinghamshire

I would have thought that Ellen would have written the inscription herself, but perhaps the handwriting was her sister's. Or Ellen's handwriting may have changed significantly in the 56 years between 1853 and 1909.

But to return to Captain William Garland. I spent many hours searching for him and eventually found him in the *Army List* for 1815, serving with the Royal Corsican Rangers. But the Royal Corsican Rangers were not at the Battle of Waterloo!

Dr Peter Boyden, Head of the Department of Archives at the National Army Museum, says: "It is not impossible that a William Garland could have served in the ranks of one of the Hussar regiments at Waterloo and subsequently received a commission after the battle".

But there is no one named Garland in the printed list of cavalrymen who served at Waterloo. And Dr Boyden's suggestion does not fit with the fact that William Garland was commissioned as a Captain in 1811, four years before the battle.

Ellen's mother, Sarah Garland (nee Shrimpton) died in 1859. So, when Ellen wrote her note about the box in 1909, she was relying on her memory of something her mother told her 50 or more years earlier. And the Battle of Waterloo was 44 years before Sarah's death.

I have reluctantly concluded that either Ellen's or her mother's memory was at fault and that, although William had served under Wellington in Spain and

Portugal, he wasn't at the Battle of Waterloo. But his box remains the Waterloo Box.

The *Army List* for 1820 gave his name among those who had died 'since last publication', and I searched the Beaconsfield parish registers for his burial without success. By chance, I spotted it in the registers for Penn. He was only 45 when he was buried on 12 October 1818. I then found that he had been

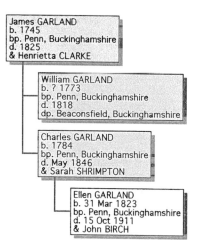

James GARLAND
b. 1745
bp. Penn, Buckinghamshire
d. 1825
& Henrietta CLARKE

William GARLAND
b. ? 1773
bp. Penn, Buckinghamshire
d. 1818
dp. Beaconsfield, Buckinghamshire

Charles GARLAND
b. 1784
bp. Penn, Buckinghamshire
d. May 1846
& Sarah SHRIMPTON

Ellen GARLAND
b. 31 Mar 1823
bp. Penn, Buckinghamshire
d. 15 Oct 1911
& John BIRCH

baptised on 15 January 1773, the son of James Garland and Henrietta Clarke. He was therefore the brother of Charles Garland, the father of Ellen, and my great-great-great uncle.

Chapter 3

Gregorys, Gilberts and Peytons

Tailor, schoolmaster, cabinet-maker and sweet-shopkeeper

My great-grandfather George Peyton Gregory lived to be 75, but his first three children all died before they were three. His fourth was my grandmother, Harriette Elizabeth, whom I have already described. The next two children, Jane Kate and Alice Mary, lived to be three years and seven weeks respectively. But the seventh child, William Frederick, was 76 when he died in 1947, and the eighth and last, Rosena Annie, reached the age of 95.

So of eight children, five died in infancy but three survived into old age. William Frederick appears in *Young, Yesterday*, as uncle Fred, but I never met him. He had two children, Peyton and Vera, at least two grandchilden, Derek and Juliet, and at least one great-grandson, Julian John Gregory, born in 1953. But I have had no contact with any of them.

Auntie Nan I do remember very clearly, a remarkable old lady with a very strongly developed bump of curiosity. She wanted to know everything about you, where you had been, what you had done, what you thought. She had the very blue Gregory eyes that my grandmother had and that Grace and my father and I inherited. She bubbled with fun and conversation.

She used to keep a sweet shop at Portishead with a huge sign over the shop window saying FRY'S CHOCOLATE, an equally large sign under the shop window saying FRY'S CHOCOLATE and quite a modest little sign over the shop door saying FRY'S CHOCOLATE. If you looked really closely, there were two other, less obtrusive signs saying 'R. A. Gregory. Confectioner.' and 'Stationery & Toys'.

Great-grandfather Gregory was a cabinet-maker. My sister has an oak bread platter and a chest of drawers, also of oak, that he made. My son Frank has his indentures: brown parchment with scarlet seals threaded on a green ribbon, a square blue stamp superimposed with silver ...

"George Peyton Gregory son of James Gregory of Milverton in the County of Warwickshire Schoolmaster ... doth put himself Apprentice. The said Apprentice his Master shall faithfully serve his secrets keep his lawful commands everywhere gladly do ... he shall not commit fornication nor contract Matrimony within the said Term shall not play at Cards or Dice Tables or any other unlawful Games whereby his said Master may have any loss ... he shall neither buy nor sell he shall not haunt Taverns or Playhouses nor absent himself from his said Master's service day or night unlawfully But in all things as a faithful Apprentice he shall behave himself towards his said Master ..."

For the first year the new apprentice was to receive four shillings a week, rising by a shilling a week to ten shillings during his seventh and final year. His master undertook to provide him with "... sufficient tools, meat, drink, lodging, physic and medical attendance and all necessaries whatsoever." The document is dated 1850.

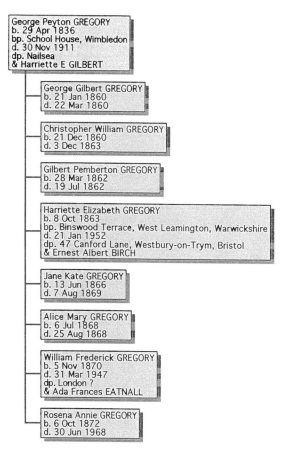

George Peyton GREGORY
b. 29 Apr 1836
bp. School House, Wimbledon
d. 30 Nov 1911
dp. Nailsea
& Harriette E GILBERT

George Gilbert GREGORY
b. 21 Jan 1860
d. 22 Mar 1860

Christopher William GREGORY
b. 21 Dec 1860
d. 3 Dec 1863

Gilbert Pemberton GREGORY
b. 28 Mar 1862
d. 19 Jul 1862

Harriette Elizabeth GREGORY
b. 8 Oct 1863
bp. Binswood Terrace, West Leamington, Warwickshire
d. 21 Jan 1952
dp. 47 Canford Lane, Westbury-on-Trym, Bristol
& Ernest Albert BIRCH

Jane Kate GREGORY
b. 13 Jun 1866
d. 7 Aug 1869

Alice Mary GREGORY
b. 6 Jul 1868
d. 25 Aug 1868

William Frederick GREGORY
b. 5 Nov 1870
d. 31 Mar 1947
dp. London ?
& Ada Frances EATNALL

Rosena Annie GREGORY
b. 6 Oct 1872
d. 30 Jun 1968

My grandmother was born at Leamington but her parents moved to Kenilworth when she was still a baby, and it was in Kenilworth that her father had his workshop, employing several men in the manufacture of sound, solid well-designed furniture. White's *Warwickshire Directory* for 1874 lists him under cabinet-makers in Kenilworth High Street.

According to Aunty Nan, he was a man of implicit integrity. Margery remembers his wearing a skull cap, a fawn frock-coat and a beard. Bernard says that in his heyday he was a great dresser. "To see him setting out for an afternoon walk in a light brown cutaway coat with an embroidered waistcoat and carrying a swordstick was quite a thing ..." The photograph I have shows a heavily beared man wearing a long coat, seated and writing at a small circular pedestal table, with a top hat on the table and an umbrella leaning against the chair. It looks posed, as it no doubt was, as it was taken by a professional photographer.

It was taken in Leamington before he and his family moved to Southsea. One of his workmen set up in competition to him in Kenilworth, undercutting his prices by using unseasoned wood, nails instead of pegs, and deal for the backs of chests. George Gregory decided on a career change and took a partenership in an auctioneer and estate agent business in Southsea. But his partner absconded with the money, and the venture was a failure.

James Gregory, tailor and schoolmaster
George Gregory's father also had a major career change. He was first a tailor and then a schoolmaster. James Gregory was born at 3am on Friday 4 November 1791 when Pitt the Younger was Prime Minister and the French Revolution was in progress. He was apprenticed to a tailor in 1805 but gave up tailoring to become a teacher.

His first child, Rosena Sarah Anne, was born at 38 Islington Terrace, now part of Cloudesley Road, London N1, but the other four children, all boys, were born at School House, Wimbledon.

The School House was built in 1758 as a charity school. By the time Betty and I visited it in 1996, it had become an independent girls' preparatory school. The building is an interesting octagonal shape and is a grade 2 listed building.

In 1832 there was a crisis of some kind at the Wimbledon Free School. The minutes of a meeting of the school committee on 17 November 1832 record that it was "resolved unanimously that this Committee after hearing and investigating the statements respecting Miss Schroeder's conduct in the school, consider it our imperative duty to remove her from the situation of School-Mistress". What on earth could the woman have done?

On 1 January 1833 the Revd Henry Lindsay reported that he had engaged Mr and Mrs Gregory, subject to the committee's confirmation, as Master and Mistress of the school, "having received very satisfactory Testimonials, as to their Character and Abilities, from persons of the highest respectability, and strong recommendations from the Committee of the Central School at Westminster".

My sister has a needlework book dated 1832 which belonged to Anne Elizabeth Gregory when she was at the Central School in the Sanctuary, Westminster, of the National Society for Promoting the Education of the Poor in the Principles of the Established Church. So that is where James and his wife were immediately before going to Wimbledon.

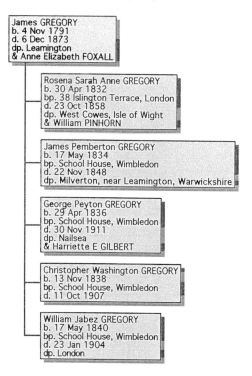

James GREGORY
b. 4 Nov 1791
d. 6 Dec 1873
dp. Leamington
& Anne Elizabeth FOXALL

Rosena Sarah Anne GREGORY
b. 30 Apr 1832
bp. 38 Islington Terrace, London
d. 23 Oct 1858
dp. West Cowes, Isle of Wight
& William PINHORN

James Pemberton GREGORY
b. 17 May 1834
bp. School House, Wimbledon
d. 22 Nov 1848
dp. Milverton, near Leamington, Warwickshire

George Peyton GREGORY
b. 29 Apr 1836
bp. School House, Wimbledon
d. 30 Nov 1911
dp. Nailsea
& Harriette E GILBERT

Christopher Washington GREGORY
b. 13 Nov 1838
bp. School House, Wimbledon
d. 11 Oct 1907

William Jabez GREGORY
b. 17 May 1840
bp. School House, Wimbledon
d. 23 Jan 1904
dp. London

Their children were neatly spaced at two-year intervals. Rosena, who was to die of typhus, came in 1832. James Pemberton Gregory was born on 17 May 1834, sharing a birthday with Margery, my Birch grandfather, and my elder grandson, James Naden. My great-grandfather arrived in 1836, followed by Christopher Washington and William Jabez Gregory in 1838 and 1840 respectively.

The first boy died, like his sister, of typhus. He was only 14, but George was 75 and Christopher and William both in their 60s when they died. I don't know much about George's younger brothers.

A new scandal
By 1841 there was a new scandal at Wimbledon Free School. *Wimbledon National Schools 1773-1912* by C T Arnold describes how a general meeting in February 1841, with the Revd Henry Lindsay again in the chair, "received a very special report from the Committee, admitting that the Gregorys had

brought the School into a bad state, but that they had resigned and that a new Master, Mr Hockridge, and a new Mistress, Miss Noad, were bringing things round".

Again one wonders just what had happened? And would Mr Hockridge and Miss Noad fare any better than the Gregorys and Miss Schroder?

So great-great-grandfather James Gregory left Wimbledon in 1841. He was at Milverton, Warwickshire, in 1850 when George's indentures were signed, and he was in Charlotte Terrace, Cowper Road, in the Parish of Hornsey in the County of Middlesex, when he signed his short will in 1858, leaving all he possessed to his "dear wife Anne Elizabeth Gregory absolutely". He died at Leamington in 1873; his wife two years later and three miles away at Kenilworth.

A small stone in Kenilworth churchyard is inscribed:

IN
memory
of
Anne Elizabeth Gregory
widow of James Gregory
of Leamington
Died Oct 25th 1875
Aged 77 years
So He giveth His Beloved sleep

I have a letter written to her from Weymouth on August Bank Holiday Monday that year, two months before her death, by her granddaughter, my grandmother, aged 11. The envelope, with a Queen Victoria one penny stamp, is addressed in my grandmother's handwriting to Mrs Gregory at Malt House Lane, Kenilworth, and my great-great-grandmother has written on it 'My Granddaughter 1st letter'.

James Gregory's father, another James, and his grandfather Joshua were both joiners at Baslow in Derbyshire. Joshua died on 16 May 1797, his wife Ann on 29 August 1789. James the elder's wife was Sarah.

The Peytons, the Gilberts, the Woodwards and the Ellises

It is now becoming difficult to see from ground level some of the higher branches of the family tree. Anne Elizabeth may have been a Peyton before she married James Gregory but it seems more likely that she was a Foxall. She had an uncle called George Peyton, who was probably her mother's brother. He was a well-to-do veterinary surgeon in Brentwood, Essex, and left her a lot of money.

His will, "contained in seven sheets of paper", was made in 1855. It is quite complicated and difficult to follow for it names more than 20 people, and it is not easy to work out their relationships. But he left his housekeeper £500 and scattered numerous larger legacies in various directions, adding up to more than £5,500. Worth rather more today. And the Peyton surname became a middle name for my great-grandfather, my father and me.

My grandmother's mother was a Gilbert, Harriette Gilbert, the eldest daughter of John Gilbert, a waiter of Maxloke, near Rugby. Or it may have been Maxtoke: my grandmother did not always cross her t's. But Rugby Library knows of no village called Maxloke or Maxtoke. The best they can come up with is Maxstoke, and that is nearer to Coleshill or Birmingham than to Rugby!

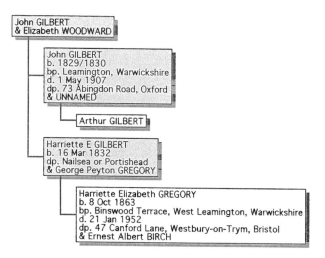

John GILBERT
& Elizabeth WOODWARD

John GILBERT
b. 1829/1830
bp. Leamington, Warwickshire
d. 1 May 1907
dp. 73 Abingdon Road, Oxford
& UNNAMED

Arthur GILBERT

Harriette E GILBERT
b. 16 Mar 1832
dp. Nailsea or Portishead
& George Peyton GREGORY

Harriette Elizabeth GREGORY
b. 8 Oct 1863
bp. Binswood Terrace, West Leamington, Warwickshire
d. 21 Jan 1952
dp. 47 Canford Lane, Westbury-on-Trym, Bristol
& Ernest Albert BIRCH

According to a note in my grandmother's unmistakable but sometimes difficult-to-read handwriting, her mother's great-uncle had an inn and a large farm at Maxloke (Maxtoke?) or at Dunchurch and owned one or two coaches which ran to Rugby. He also had two daughters. Jane married the village schoolmaster, Mr Berry, and Mary Ann married Mr Sutton, a farmer, who lived at the bottom of the hill.

A yellowing cutting from the *Oxford Chronicle* for 3 May 1907 records the death of Mr John Gilbert, "a man of singular ability, esteemed among his friends and fellow-workers". This was Harriette Gregory's brother. He was born in Leamington in 1829 or 1830 and moved to Oxford in 1865 as Goods Superintendent to the Great Western Railway Company, a position he occupied for more than 30 years.

He had three sons and a daughter and, presumably, had had a wife, but his obituary makes no mention of her.

As we have seen, my Birch grandmother's mother was Harriette Gilbert before she married George Peyton Gregory. *Her* mother was Elizabeth Woodward. Elizabeth had a sister, Jane.

My sister has three samplers, one made in 1812 by Elizabeth Woodward when Napoleon was retreating from Moscow and she was aged nine, the other made by Jane Woodward in 1821 when she was 14. The third by Harriet Woodward is undated. She may have been a sister of Jane and Elizabeth or perhaps their mother.

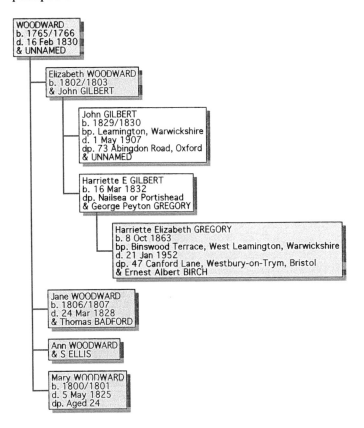

I have a scrap of paper on which Elizabeth (or possibly another sister Ann) has listed the births, marriages and deaths of her immediate relations between 1825 and 1830. This Ann married a Mr S Ellis on 11 December 1826, and they had three children, Jane, Fanny and John.

Half a century later John Ellis and his wife Annie were living in the Cornish fishing village of Portscatho, a few doors away from John's sister Fanny. John was a school manager, secretary and treasurer of the Gerrans, Philleigh and St

Anthony District Nursing Association, secretary of the Portscatho Reading Room, and secretary and treasurer of the Lighting Committee.He was "a fine looking gentleman with a handsome beard", Margery was told.

John and Annie Ellis lived in Portscatho for 21 years. His obituary in the local paper was headed 'A Loss to the Community' and began: "It was with the keenest regret that all at Portscatho received intelligence of the death of Mr. John Ellis, who passed away on Thursday of last week at the age of 75 years."

Elizabeth Woodward's father was born about 1765, James Garland in 1745, and the first John Birch about 1736. I can tell you about my mother's family as far back as the 1650s.

Chapter 4

My mother

From the mountains of St Kitts,
via Trinidad and Barbados,
to the fells of Cumbria
in England

My mother's family has been in the Caribbean for three and a half centuries. She was born on 28 September 1905 in St Kitts, the mother colony of what was then the British West Indies. Her birth took place on Brighton Estate in the parish of St Mary, but I'm not sure what her mother was doing there.

As a child, I was given to understand that my mother had been christened at St John's, Fig Tree, in the neighbouring island of Nevis, where Nelson's marriage certificate is displayed.

Her father was working as Revenue Officer in Nevis in 1905, but I have been unable to find any record of her baptism there or in St Kitts.

As a little girl, Iris Berkeley King went to a dame school in Basseterre, where she was taught to write and do sums on a slate and learned by rote the kings and queens of England and the cities and rivers of Europe.

Quarter of a century later, I went to the same school and was taught to write and do sums on a slate and learned by rote the kings and queens of England and the cities and rivers of Europe.

Berkeley is a family name. Iris' great-grandmother was a Berkeley, from "one of the branches of the ancient and illustrious house of Berkeley in the county of Gloucestershire" according to a memorial tablet in the church of St George in Basseterre.

I don't know why she was called Iris.

One night in 1910, when she was four, she and her brother Bryan were woken by their father and taken outside the house to see Halley's comet. It would be a once-in-a-lifetime experience, he told them. But seventy six years later she saw it a second time, standing with her Zimmer frame in her back garden at Cockermouth in Cumbria, where a local astronomer had kindly erected his telescope especially for her.

When Iris was ten, her little sister Milly died, aged only five, and this greatly affected her. She was not, my sister believes, helped to grieve. In fact, she was so distressed that her distress upset her mother, and Iris was sent away to the country.

This may have helped her mother; it is doubtful if it helped her. When she was older, she was sent to the Girls' High School in Antigua, where she

33

played cricket. She was a tomboy and a great climber of trees. In later life she took up rifle range shooting in St Kitts and became a first-class shot. She was awarded the Bell medal of the Society of Miniature Rifle Clubs. So that she could use her better eye when aiming, she had to buy a 'left-handed' rifle. Sadly, she wasn't allowed to bring it into England unless she joined a rifle club, and this she couldn't afford to do.

Iris had wanted to be a doctor, but she was a girl and her parents were poor, and there was no way that she could get to medical school. Her younger brother was the very first student to win the Leeward Islands scholarship, and he went to Cambridge. But presumably that opportunity was not open to her. Her first job was as a bank clerk with the Royal Bank of Canada in Basseterre.

Then in 1923 my father was transferred to St Kitts, they fell in love and were married at St George's, Basseterre. Iris liked things plain and simple, no fuss. So it was a very simple wedding in the morning with just a few family and friends. The bride did not wear a wedding dress, just a plain white linen suit. According to a bystander outside the church, presumably disappointed by the small congregation and lack of flowers and finery, it was a 'miserable' wedding. But I believe it to have been a very happy marriage.

And miserable wedding or not, there was certainly a wedding cake, as I still have one of the minute cards printed in silver ink "With Mr. and Mrs. N. Peyton Birch's Compliments, St Kitts, B.W.I., June 7th 1927" and sent out with pieces of wedding cake in little white boxes.

They lived initially at Marine Villa, 'down at the Fort', or Fortlands as it is now called. That's where I was born ten months after the wedding. "Mr. and Mrs. N. Peyton Birch announce the birth of Christopher Berkeley on 26th April 1928. Weight 9lbs." said the little card posted across the Atlantic for a penny ha'penny to my Aunt Con at Guildhall, Bristol.

Iris was, for her time, a modern and progressive mother. She followed the teachings of Dr Marie Stopes as set out in *Married Love* and *Wise Parenthood*. Because of Dr Frederic Truby King's *Feeding and Care of Baby*, my sister and I were fed by the clock and not on demand. I do not know what effect this unnatural practice had on us.

When my sister was born four years later, we were living at Avondale, just off Pall Mall Square, now Independence Square, in the heart of Basseterre. We later moved to Rozelle, near the Tennis Club, which my parents belonged to.

Iris also had a great love for cricket. In later years, when she watched the test matches on television, she would turn the sound off and listen instead to the commentary on her Roberts radio.

In 1938 my parents moved from St Kitts to Trinidad. My mother's passport, issued by the Governor and Commander-in-Chief in and over the Colony of Trinidad and Tobago, says that her hair was brown and her eyes hazel and that she had no special peculiarities. In fact, she was a handsome woman.

Trinidad and Barbados

Housekeeping in Trinidad during the war years was no joke. On very special occasions when we were entertaining, perhaps an airman from the Fleet Air Arm's training base at Piarco, she would open *two* tins of meat, using corned beef as a base for shepherd's pie and then dotting the top with sausages.

Some of the family silver was given to help buy a Spitfire for the Royal Air Force. She joined the Women's Voluntary Service, and very smart she looked in her dark green uniform. The WVS in Trinidad cared for the many merchant seamen whose ships had been torpedoed by U-boats operating in the Caribbean.

Her four years in Barbados immediately after the war were, I think, somewhat less stressful.

Despite all their problems, my parents loved each other. Certainly, when my father died in 1950, my mother was so distressed that she exercised a widow's prerogative not to attend her husband's funeral.

Widowhood in England

After my father's death, she first went to Liverpool to stay with her friend Mindie, the daughter of Archdeacon Jullion who had married her at St George's 23 years earlier. Mother then moved to London, sharing a flat at Notting Hill Gate with Daphne Shepherd. I and my new wife took over the flat in 1951, when Mother returned to St Kitts to care for her father who was dying.

She had been active in the Girl Guide movement in St Kitts in the 1930s and became involved again in the 1950s. It seems that she was asked to form a Girl Guide company and, when it transpired that it would be for white girls only, she refused.

In the St Kitts years, before moving to Trinidad, swimming at Frigate Bay, then the private beach of Sir Wilfred and Lady Wigley, was a regular Sunday fixture. In the 1950s she took up snorkelling. When she was nearly 50, she learned to drive and, after she had passed her test, her younger brother allowed her to use his car. Neither she nor her husband ever owned a car.

When she came back to England, she got a job on the housekeeping staff of Badminton School in Bristol and was working there when her first grandchild was born in January 1954. In fact Frank had been expected on Stalin's birthday, 21 December, and Mother came up to London to our Holland Road flat to help look after me over Christmas while Betty was giving birth. But Frank was late, not arriving until 5 January. By that time Mother had had to return to work.

She went out to St Kitts again to look after her mother and was there during the Hungarian uprising in October 1956, when Betty and I and our two children were in Budapest. She wrote to us, care of Betty's mother in Northamptonshire, on 30 October 1956: "I have been simply terrified since I last wrote - almost in a panic, as things sounded so much worse since I had your reassuring cable. Some days I've been sick with fear and then at other times I feel that you must be alright. Now today I hear that the Russians have withdrawn from the centre of Budapest. I am very annoyed with the BBC as they are now putting Egypt and Israel first on the news and Budapest is taking about third place. What a difference it makes when you are personally interested."

My grandmother died in February 1958, and later that year Mother crossed the Atlantic for the last time. To begin with, she stayed in a friend's flat in London, and then rented a flat in West Kensington. She subsequently lived in Hampstead, Richmond and Putney, and suffered increasingly from fits of depression. At that time my sister was living with her and worked at St Stephen's Hospital, where she was a pioneer of play therapy on the children's ward.

My mother and my sister had had several holidays in the Lake District. Mother loved the fells, as they reminded her of the beautiful mountains in St Kitts. She seemed so much happier in Cumbria than in London that my sister, who had inherited some money from her aunt Con, gave up her job at St Stephen's and bought a small house in Cockermouth. They moved there in 1981.They had been looking forward to walking among the fells, but this pleasure was short lived.

Mother's eyesight began to fail. She had had a cataract operation before they left London. She had a second cataract operation soon after moving to the Lake District, and was still waiting for her new glasses when she contracted meningitis. No one thought she would recover. But she did. By this time she was developing osteoporosis.

Then came Alzheimer's. Although the disease had been discovered in 1906, for an incredible seven decades there was little or no information or support for the families and carers of people with Alzheimer's. The Alzheimer's Society was not founded until 1979. Mother became more and more forgetful; her GP told my sister that his memory was also bad. No one mentioned dementia or Alzheimer's. My sister struggled as best she could to look after Mother, but it was heart-breaking work. It was never going to be easy but, with the information and support available today, it might have been a little less difficult.

I spent my 60th birthday sitting with Mother as she lay unconscious in the West Cumberland Hospital. She died in the early hours of the next day, 27 April 1988. She was 82.

Chapter 5

Bryan, also known as Rufus

'The third finest legal brain in Europe'

My King grandparents had five children. My mother was their first. Bryan Earle was their second, arriving just 14 months after my mother. Bryan and Earle were both family names. His grandmother was a Bryan, and *her* great-grandmother was an Earle. But, because of his red hair, he was always known in St Kitts and to his family as Rufus. In England, where he spent 50 years of his life, he was Bryan to his friends and B E King to his academic colleagues.

I owe a lot to him. He paid for my university education and eventually made me his executor and residuary legatee. He was an interesting man and had an interesting life. His obituary ran to 28 inches in the local paper and 11 inches in *The Times*.

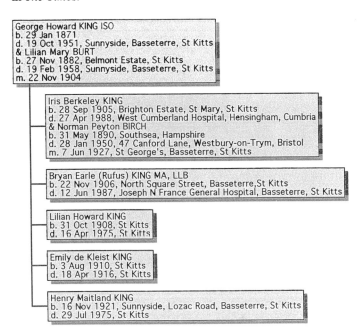

George Howard KING ISO
b. 29 Jan 1871
d. 19 Oct 1951, Sunnyside, Basseterre, St Kitts
& Lilian Mary BURT
b. 27 Nov 1882, Belmont Estate, St Kitts
d. 19 Feb 1958, Sunnyside, Basseterre, St Kitts
m. 22 Nov 1904

Iris Berkeley KING
b. 28 Sep 1905, Brighton Estate, St Mary, St Kitts
d. 27 Apr 1988, West Cumberland Hospital, Hensingham, Cumbria
& Norman Peyton BIRCH
b. 31 May 1890, Southsea, Hampshire
d. 28 Jan 1950, 47 Canford Lane, Westbury-on-Trym, Bristol
m. 7 Jun 1927, St George's, Basseterre, St Kitts

Bryan Earle (Rufus) KING MA, LLB
b. 22 Nov 1906, North Square Street, Basseterre, St Kitts
d. 12 Jun 1987, Joseph N France General Hospital, Basseterre, St Kitts

Lilian Howard KING
b. 31 Oct 1908, St Kitts
d. 16 Apr 1975, St Kitts

Emily de Kleist KING
b. 3 Aug 1910, St Kitts
d. 18 Apr 1916, St Kitts

Henry Maitland KING
b. 16 Nov 1921, Sunnyside, Lozac Road, Basseterre, St Kitts
d. 29 Jul 1975, St Kitts

He was sent to the Antigua Grammar School and was, in 1923, the very first student to win the Leeward Islands scholarship. He went up to Cambridge in 1924 to read law at Pembroke College. Why he chose Pembroke, I do not know, but his birthday, 22 November, was possibly the birthday of the Countess of Pembroke, who had founded the college in 1347. It was certainly an important date for her as she is depicted wearing her marital coat of arms against that date in her Book of Hours. But Rufus is unlikely to have known that at the time, so there must have been some other reason. Perhaps Pembroke chose him. Tony Camps, a former Master of the college, suggested that Pembroke may have offered him a place on the basis of his performance in the Higher Certificate examination run by the Oxford and Cambridge Joint Board.

If that was so, the college's judgment was vindicated when, in 1926, he was the only undergraduate placed in the first division of the first class in part I of the law tripos, winning the George Long Prize for Roman law. He was one of only six, in 1927, in the first division of the first class in part II. A year later, when he was only 21, he was elected a Fellow of his college.

His undergraduate years could not have been easy. His parents were poor and his scholarship was only £150 a year, which, with skimping, paid half his costs. Fortunately, he was able to get a tutoring job in the long vacation, and Mrs Aymee Bromley, an old family friend, allowed him £40 a year. Her son Antony had been killed when hunting, and she consequently 'adopted' Rufus.

He had chosen Roman law as it alone offered a prize of £25. He bought himself a pair of pink flared trousers, a purchase he later regretted but he could not afford to replace them. He believed implicitly in the value of woollen vests but nevertheless contracted bronchitis every winter.

When his parents visited him in Cambridge, a cruel limerick circulated.

> There was a young Fellow called King
> Whose parents were not quite The Thing ...

I don't know how it ended, but it must have been very hurtful.

His very first job, which he combined with his fellowship, was as assistant legal secretary to the National Confederation of Employers Organisations in 1927. In 1929 he took the bachelor of laws examination and was again placed in the first division of the first class.

He was in chambers for six months before being called to the bar in 1930, having eaten his dinners at Gray's Inn. He practised little, and his arguments were not always understood. "Are you, Mr King", he recalled Lord Goddard inquiring in court, "appearing on behalf of the defence or of the prosecution?".

Goddard's successor as Lord Chief Justice, Lord Taylor of Gosforth, had similar difficulties in following Rufus' train of thought, as did his cousin Sir Francis Burt, a former Chief Justice of Western Australia. Lord Taylor said that Rufus taught him "a brand of jurisprudence which laid great emphasis on defining such basic terms as 'right', 'duty', norm' etc; 'semantic jurisprudence' I remember calling it".

His obituary in Pembroke's *Annual Gazette* said "his lectures were difficult and ... did not secure the attendance they deserved". But Leon Brittan, now Lord Brittan of Spennithorne, attributed his first in the tripos to Rufus' "interesting lectures and stimulating supervision".

Someone said that he had the third finest legal brain in Europe, but I don't know who said so or to whom the other two brains belonged.

In 1930 he was Whewell scholar in international law and spent his scholarship year at the University of Vienna attending courses in the philosphy of law and Professor Verdross' international law seminar.

As a college fellow in the 1930s, he was active as praelector, tutor and director of studies. He was faculty lecturer in jurisprudence (1931-32), Roman law problems (1932-33), and Roman law and international relations (1933-34). He was university lecturer in Roman law and jurisprudence (1934-35), international law (1935-37), and jurisprudence (1938).

He was elected Membre Titulaire de l'Institut International de Philosophie du Droit et de Sociologie Juridique in 1934.

In the early 1930s he was strongly recommended by the Cambridge authorities to the Foreign Office for the post of legal adviser to the Foreign Office in Baghdad at a salary of £2,400 pa. But he withdrew his application at the last moment owing to deaths on the staff of his college 'which made it a duty to remain'.

While he was still in his twenties, he was offered the chair of law at Birmingham. He asked Pembroke if they would keep his fellowship open so that, if after a year he found that the Birmingham job wasn't to his liking, he could come back. I don't know whether Pembroke refused or Rufus or Birmingham had second thoughts, but he remained at Cambridge.

The 'colour problem', Sharpeville and Enoch Powell

My uncle felt deeply about the 'colour problem' as it was known before the war. He used the opportunity of his last lecture on international law, given in Cambridge's magnificent Senate House as his usual lecture room was under repair, to demand the expulsion of South Africa from the Commonwealth. And that was in 1937.

After the Sharpeville massacre in 1960, Rufus organised an Apartheid Relief Fund in Cambridge. He contributed £100, the vice-chancellor gave £50, and the Kittitians in Birmingham passed round the hat and sent £20. Altogether £1000 was raised. The money was sent to South Africa and used to send a black engineer and a black medical student to England for further education.

Both he and Enoch Powell were members of the exclusive Carlyle Club. After Powell's notorious 'rivers of blood' speech in 1968, Rufus wrote to him: "Dear Enoch, ... I regard the West Indies as Britain's Southern States. Geography has made it possible for Britain to deal with the West Indies in a way different from that in which the North has dealt with the South in the USA. To enforce the geographical barrier by a legal one I regard as moral cowardice and a confession of national failure.... This then is the charge against which you have to clear yourself, before your conscience, God and History. That you have made your 'voluntary' repatriation scheme an evil mockery -- a fleeing from your self-fulfilling prophecy of the wrath to come..."

A close friend at this time was J W F Rowe, who had been elected a fellow of Pembroke in 1934. He gave Rufus a silver cigarette box with his (Rowe's) initials on it.

Rufus acted *in loco parentis* for various children from St Kitts at school in England, notably his much younger brother Harry, who was at Aldenham School when war broke out, and his cousin Lynn, who died of a brain tumour at the same school in 1938. During the 1930s he served on the executive of the London-based West India Committee and represented St Kitts on the Colonial Office Sugar Advisory Committee.

At the start of the war he became a Local Defence Volunteer (precursor of the Home Guard) in order to defend Cambridge against the invading Germans. But he soon moved to London, living in Oxford House in Bethnal Green and working for the Home Office (Children's Branch) and the Ministry of Aircraft Production. The Oxford House report for 1943-1944 lists Bryan King as one of ten voluntary workers.

It was during his time with the Home Office that he acquired an interest in the problem of juvenile delinquency, and he was largely responsible for establishing Kneesworth Hall, an approved school for intelligent young criminals at Royston, near Cambridge. For many years he was a governor of the school, serving with Lady Adrian, the mother of Richard Adrian who later became the Master of Pembroke and presided over the admission in 1983 of women to the college. This was something to which Rufus had been strongly opposed.

With the British Council in Barbados

Towards the end of the war, the British Council started setting up offices in the West Indies, and early in 1945 Rufus flew out to Trinidad, where I, my sister and my parents were living, and then on to Barbados to become the first British Council representative in that colony. He told me that he had written a letter of resignation after his first day in office, but he stayed on until 1946. Many years later when I was researching at the Public Record Office at Kew, I came across some British Council files and looked to see what there was about his time in Barbados. I found a note, saying that his first (and only) annual report for 1945 had been destroyed as its retention was not in the council's interest.

In 1946 he returned to Cambridge in the expectation of being given a senior position at Pembroke but this did not happen. Only his tenure as Pembroke's director of studies in law was resumed together with his university lectureship in jurisprudence. He became disenchanted with mainstream law and increasingly preoccupied with jurisprudence and philosophy, and in 1952 Tony Camps, as tutor, relieved him of the job of director of studies in law. This is what I have been told by Rufus' successor as director of studies in law.

The minutes of College Meetings tell a slightly different, but not necessarily more accurate, story. According to Sir Roger Tomkys, the present Master, "on 22 May 1951 the Governing Body agreed, at Bryan King's request, that he should continue for a further year as Director of Studies in Law but with a minimal teaching load and also that 12 months later another Director of Studies in Law should be appointed".

Rufus wrote to a friend: "I have rid myself of responsibility for the college's teaching of law -- and £400 a year -- but have nevertheless been re-elected to a non-stipendiary fellowship, with nothing to live on but a good deal more liberty to follow my own thoughts and inclinations. Of course I remain university lecturer in jurisprudence -- one can only be sacked from that in case of crime".

He was, of course, exaggerating when he suggested that as a non-stipendiary fellow he would have had nothing to live on. His university lectureship would have been his principal source of income. However, I don't think Rufus ever forgave Camps, although he confessed to me that he no longer knew what the law was all about. But he knew that he was a West Indian, although he was white and had lived most of his life in England; he knew that West Indian culture was his culture; that the West Indian people were his people.

He counted among his friends the black peers Lords Constantine and Pitt and the West Indian prime ministers Norman Manley, Forbes Burnham, Grantley Adams and Robert Bradshaw. Also the West Indian writers George Lamming, Edward Kamau Brathwaite and H A Vaughan and the Trinidadian painter Dermot Louison. Brathwaite's first long poem *Mulatto,* written in Cambridge, is dedicated to Rufus. His rooms at Pembroke, occupied in the 18th century first by Thomas Gray, the poet, and then by William Pitt the Younger, were like a museum of West Indian art and crafts. They are described in Lamming's novel *The Emigrants.*

In 1956 some West Indian editors visited Cambridge, and Rufus entertained them in his rooms. The Jamaican editor said: "Mr King, I see St Kitts coming up all the time. It's St Kitts, St Kitts, St Kitts. Have you ever been there?".

The 1948 sugar plantation strike
He had indeed. Quite apart from the little matter of having been born there, he had flown back, at his own expense, in 1948 to help negotiate a settlement to a major strike by the sugar plantation workers. Ivan Weekes' account of the strike, *The Dawn of a Gloomy Day*, describes Rufus as "this unadulterated

gentleman, the Saviour of the people of St Kitts-Nevis, the spice of justice".

In his foreword to the book, which he hadn't yet read, Rufus wrote: "No one had asked for my assistance. But I had wanted to give it; I had been allowed to give it; and it had been all too generously acknowledged. I could now look at those men returning to work, with a heart almost unbearably full, and feel that at last I had been able to render some small service to the island which had sent me overseas to be trained for a profession".

He was 'mentioned in despatches' by Earl Baldwin, Governor of the Leeward Islands, for his "great work in ending the 13 week sugar strike of 1948".

He also did much for West Indian students and artists in Britain. According to *The Times'* obituarist, "to countless immigrants King became an unofficial godfather". He helped set up the West Indian Students Centre in Earl's Court, London, and was chairman of its board from 1963 to 1969.

The British Council sent him to Nigeria on a lecture tour in December1951 / January 1952. He lectured in all the bigger towns and described it as his 'great adventure', hoping that it would enable him 'to play a little part in helping Nigerians' in England.

He enthusiastically supported Les Ballets Negres, Europe's first black dance company, formed in 1946 by Richie Riley and Berto Pasuka. When they came to Cambridge in 1952, he entertained them in his rooms and helped out of his own pocket when there wasn't enough money for their wages.

Like several of the dancers, Rufus was homosexual, but largely if not entirely chaste. He told me that he was not a practising homosexual as he could not find anyone to practise with. When I wrote to tell him that I too was gay, he burnt my letter. That was in the dark pre-Wolfenden days of illegality. In 1963 Rufus went out to St Kitts, as his brother Harry was ill and needed his help. He spent four weeks up in the mountains with Harry and his 18-year-old negro house-boy, Malachi. Rufus described what he called his 'honeymoon with Malachi' in an amazing 18-page essay of lust, guilt and chastity. Although their relationship was chaste, Alan Hollinghurst, the gay novelist and assistant editor of *The Times Literary Supplement,* found the manuscript "well written, touching and extremely sexy".

In 1964 one of Rufus' friends died as a result of a bizarre accident. The *Daily Telegraph* described how he was found "lying dead on the floor, with a rope tied in a slip-knot around his neck .... dressed in a black sweater and black ballet tights pulled up only to the buttocks ... a small gold-coloured chain around the left ankle, underneath the tights". After the accident, the widow asked Rufus to take away the chains, padlocks, straps and other things that were found in the dead man's bedroom. These Rufus kept under his bed in Cambridge for some time until he fell ill and, fearing that he might die and not wanting them to be found under his bed, asked me to remove them.

After his retirement to St Kitts a local rag carried two scurrilous pargraphs under the heading IS IT TRUE? "That after reading the *Labour Latrine* for last Saturday, people are saying that Lee Moore should step down and let Bryan King take over the decrepit Labour Party? That people are now calling the Labour Party the 'GAY' party because of the two regular writers in the *Labour Spokesman* (the mouthpiece of the Labour Party) whose christian names begin with the letter 'B'?" Rufus was livid and threatened to sue for libel until dissuaded by George Walker, the former Archdeacon of St Kitts.

As his obituary in the *Pembroke College Annual Gazette* noted, Rufus was 'a handsome tall man'. In fact he was nearly 6ft 4in. Several women (and a few men) fell in love with him. To one woman friend he wrote: "I am very touched by your letter, a little distressed and humiliated (or made to feel humble), though not altogether surprised. You have been so thoughtful and considerate for some little time that you have made me feel quite ashamed of my own selfishness.

"What makes me distressed is the thought that you may be feeling lonely at times, and wanting someone to look after-- what makes me feel humble is that you should want to look after me. But no one can -- not even myself. Or at least I am far too selfish to allow anyone else even to try.

"I should feel quite lost without my ailments and grouses and excuses. And I treasure them too dearly to run the risk of losing them. Where *would* I be if I went to Majorca and got cured of my bronchitis? I should lose my dearest possession. Very complicated -- or just a simple fraud?".

The Caribbean Artists Movement
Rufus was very much involved with the Caribbean Artists Movement, formed in 1966 by Brathwaite, John La Rose and Andrew Salkey. As chairman of the West Indian Students' Centre, Rufus was able to make the centre available to CAM for some of its meetings. He took the chair at a CAM lecture in July 1967 given by C L R James, and he, James and Frank Collymore were made honorary members of CAM.

Rufus liked to be at the centre of attention; he was an exhibitionist; he became increasingly eccentric as he grew older. He confessed that, as a student, he had always specialised in the most difficult subject as a way of drawing attention to himself. In 1965 he wrote to his brother: "I get ruder and ruder to people and say the most outrageous things that I don't really mean".

Lord Taylor says that Rufus was "undoubtedly eccentric but extremely charming" and that "he could draw a longer stretch of cigarette in one intake of breath than anyone I've ever met". Mr Justice Rougier says that he was "an extremely friendly and courteous eccentric, of a type we sorely need".

Lunching with my mother and sister at the Royal Commonwealth Society and elsewhere, he would cause them considerable embarrassment by raising his voice until the entire restaurant was listening. After dining in college at high table, he would lie down on the floor of the senior parlour and perform the stretching exercises for which he became notable in later life.

These were necessary, Rufus said, because of a back problem resulting from a fall from a horse when he was a boy. Be that as it may, he was convinced that the way to cure it was to perform a strange circular dance, twisting his body, preferably but not necessarily to music, preferably but not necessarily in public. This too could be pretty embarrassing for anyone with him at the time.

On election day in February 1974, he demonstrated on Market Hill, Cambridge, bearing a placard saying: BURDENS HAVE ALWAYS FALLEN ON THOSE LEAST ABLE TO BEAR THEM. CONSERVATIVE MOTTO. VOTE THEM OUT. Warmly wrapped against the cold and wearing a large straw hat, he was accompanied by a small steel band made up of the children of a St Kitts fisherman, Kenneth Ramsey, and his photograph duly appeared in the *Cambridge Evening News*.

Rufus later said that he would have had the Conservative MP unseated if his nine-year-old drummer had not had such bad toothache that Rufus had had to take him to a dentist and the rest of the band had then disappeared.

The Ramsey family was very important to Rufus, as he was to them. There were four sons and a daughter. Two of them were born in St Kitts and three in England. All of them, except for one son, made music with their father. They visited Rufus every Sunday for tea and a walk. He took them to the park, and derived much pleasure from playing with the children. He was like a grandfather to them, giving them a lot of his time and helping financially as well. He probably had a closer domestic relationship with them than with anyone else.

He had now spent nearly 50 years in Cambridge, and it would soon be time to go home. His university appointment was due to expire at the end of September. He had written no books but he had contributed 'Prescription of Claims in International Law' to the *British Year Book of International Law* and British cases to the *Annual Digest of Public International Law Cases*. And he wrote reviews for the *Law Quarterly Review, Journal of the Society of Comparative Legislation, International Affairs, Journal of the Society of Public Teachers of Law, Cambridge Law Journal,* and *New Commonwealth Quarterly*. He also wrote innumerable letters to *The Times*, some of which were published.

A memorial in Westminster Abbey

He presented the college with a pair of Georgian silver sauce boats. But he wanted to do something else to express his gratitude to his college for having provided him with board and lodging for half a century, and he hit on the idea of putting up a memorial to the college's foundress in Westminster Abbey near her husband's tomb.

He did some research, collected some material and produced some rough sketches. His design was based on the portrait of St Cecilia with the Countess of Pembroke taken from her Book of Hours. He envisaged it being executed in the finest enamel and reversed so that, when placed at the doorway into the Chapel of Our Lady of the Pew, which she was thought to have founded, the Countess would be seen looking at her husband's tomb. The eventual design and siting of the memorial was quite different, but that is another story.

Westminster Abbey's Librarian and Keeper of the Muniments was Lawrence Tanner who had been at Pembroke from 1909 to 1912, occupying rooms in Ivy Court immediately beneath the rooms where Rufus later lived. Tanner had written an article in the *Pembroke College Annual Gazette* in 1959 about the Chapel of Our Lady of the Pew which ended with his saying "one could wish, now that the connection of this little chapel with our Foundress and her husband is known, that it could be more closely identified with the college which bears their name".

Consequently, Rufus wrote to Tanner about his idea for a memorial in the Abbey and, at Tanner's suggestion, to Edward Carpenter, who had just become Dean of Westminster. And Dean Carpenter wrote to the Master of Pembroke, Tony Camps, who hastily explained that the proposed memorial was entirely King's idea and responsibility and nothing whatever to do with the college. There the matter rested when Rufus retired and returned to St Kitts in 1974.

At his last big college feast, he was allowed to invite one guest, so he invited three: the Commissioner for the Eastern Caribbean, Oswald Gibbs, Lord Alport, a former pupil, and Lord Walston. He was not supposed to make a speech, but he did. He said: "You British, you know how to murder, how to enslave, how to exploit and then leave to starve. But until you learn how to live with, you are a nation doomed". He then went on to say that he was personally responsible for 29 St Kitts babies in Cambridge and that he wouldn't be happy until 5% of the population of England were of African descent.

The college generously granted Rufus full facilities for a farewell garden party, and this was held on 20 July. He invited 80 West Indians from Birmingham, including a cricket XI and a steel band, and another 40 from London, including another cricket XI, and there were about 20 West Indians from Cambridge.

Also present were the Jamaican High Commissioner, the Eastern Caribbean High Commissioner, Sir Hugh Springer and Sir Roy Marshal from Barbados, the Liberian Ambassador to the United Nations, and the Mayor of Cambridge. Rufus' rooms with his West Indian books and pictures and his collection of illustrations of the negro in art were on show, together with a photographic exhibition illustrating aspects of 18th century West Indian life and contrasting the work of William Blake and Agostino Brunias in depicting slave society.

There were cricket matches between teams from the West Indian Students Centre and the St Christopher Association of Birmingham on the Pembroke

College grounds and between the Cambridge West Indians and their opponents in the local league on Parker's Piece.

In the evening there was a dance at the University Centre with the St Christopher's Steel Band from Birmingham. At midnight, after God Save the Queen, the leader of the band rose and said: "The glorious sunshine today, the wonderful cricket matches, and all the sweetness we have put into our music was all for Mr King".

As the band, which normally charged £100, had come for only £30, Rufus searched all round London until he found, at Asprey's, seven St Christopher medals, enamel on silver, and sent a medal to each of the players.

Back to St Kitts

The party over, it was time to pack and return home. His Barbadian friend Antony Haynes, who had been at Pembroke just after the war and who was then running Booker Brothers, gave him a free passage on a sugar boat back to the West Indies.

Shortly after his return to St Kitts, he sent the Pembroke College porters a postcard to say that he had been arrested for hitting a policeman and then released so that he could attend a garden party at Government House.

During the next 13 years his back problem seemed to get worse, although he was always confident that it would be better in a day or two. In 1977 he wrote to a friend: "My back has been morally incapacitating as well as physically and I have in fact done nothing for months while undone duties piled up". In 1983 he wrote to my mother: "My dear Iris, I booked a ticket to the UK two months ago and haven't been able to move since. Luckily I realised that night that I couldn't cope with it in three days time and cancelled it the next day, so that I only forfeited the deposit".

When Betty and I visited him later that year, he was spending most of the time lying naked, or almost naked, on his verandah. But he managed to walk into the centre of Basseterre with us. I say 'walk' but it was more like a dance, inevitably attracting a certain amount of public interest.

In addition to his back, his principal concerns during retirement were the need for a national museum on the island and the fight against the form of constitution which the British government was seeking to impose on St Kitts and Nevis.

In 1974, while still in Cambridge, he had written to his friend Robert Bradshaw, Premier of the Associated State, describing his vision of the museum. "I would like it to be more than a purely local or even Caribbean museum, but include the sort of display of the English and French and African culture which would illustrate the historical background of our tradition."

Rufus came back to England for the last time in September 1976. Where he went and what he did in the five and a half weeks he was here, I know not. But immediately after his return to St Kitts in October, he began to plan and prepare for the exhibition that he hoped would give a taste of what a national museum might be like.

I was on the other side of the Atlantic, and it is not easy to piece together what happened. There was a committee, with Rufus as chairman, but it seems that it did not survive the difficulties of organising the sort of exhibition that Rufus wanted. The committee and / or Rufus were fortunate in securing the use of the Georgian House on the south side of what used to be Pall Mall Square and is now Independence Square.

A hundred years earlier this had been the town house of Rufus' great grandfather, Thomas Probyn Berridge, and was in many ways eminently suitable. The exhibition was entitled 'Two Artists Who Came and Went', Isobel Badcock who visited St Kitts in 1923 and Dermot Louison, a much more recent visitor. The title chosen was a reference to *The People Who Came*, Longman's secondary school history for the Caribbean. The book was also widely used in English schools at that time.

It was felt that 'The People Who Came' should be the theme of the national museum, which it was hoped would be established. Originally, the exhibition was to be in just one room but as Rufus' ideas grew so did the size of the exhibition. It filled two, then three, then four and finally all the rooms of the large house.

Rufus wanted to celebrate St Kitts as the Mother of the Antilles, both British and French, with Sir Thomas Warner's charter and tomb and Phillipe de Longvilliers de Poincy's costume and palace. There were to be exhibits illustrating the historic and artistic relation between *The Sable Venus* by Thomas Stothard and *Europe supported by Africa & America* by William Blake and their relation to Botticelli's Madonnas. And there were also to be pictures depicting the history of the people of St Kitts with a photograph of the island from the moon, Michaelangelo's *Creation of Adam*, a 17th century French *Adam and Eve*, both Caribs, the male wearing nothing at all and the female a pawpaw leaf, Columbus and his ship and a glimpse such as he might have had of St Kitts.

I don't know how much of this was achieved. The day chosen for the official opening by the Premier, 15 December 1976, turned out to be Budget Day, so Robert Bradshaw was unable to attend. However, the Governor stepped into the breach at the last moment, but to no avail. Pictures that Rufus had spent six hours putting up were taken down so that the room concerned could be painted. For Rufus this was the last straw, he disappeared, and the committee placed a notice on the door of the house, saying 'Opening of the Exhibition Postponed'.

An hour an a half later, Rufus reappeared, tore down the notice and opened the exhibition himself.

It seems that the exhibition ran for several months. An article in *The Demo-*

crat for 9 April 1977 said: "The dream of Professor Brian King (sic) is a National Museum in which the drama of the history of St Kitts will unfold against the wider world of which St Kitts is merely a part, albeit an exciting part ... we are to thank Mr King for this majestic dream."

For the first three years of the 1980s, Rufus was preoccupied with the fast approaching independence of his island home and the constitutional proposals for this, which he thought were gravely flawed.

He spoke at public meetings attended by crowds of 6,000 to 9,000, wrote articles and leaflets, composed verses, addressed a petition to the Queen and appealed to his many friends and acquaintances in the House of Commons and the House of Lords.

The chief defect, in his eyes, of the proposed constitution was that there was no provision for any elected representative body for St Kitts itself other than the Federal Assembly, while Nevis would have its own separate legislature. This inferior position in the new Federal State was not one from which St Kitts could escape by secession, though secession was to be allowed to Nevis. Thus the people of St Kitts would be locked into a straight-jacket of which Nevis would be given the key.

When the order to end the status of association between the United Kingdom and the Associated State of St Christopher and Nevis was debated in the House of Lords, Lord Pitt, briefed by me, put forward Rufus' views. But the UK was more anxious to get rid of the St Kitts-Nevis problem than to solve it. St Kitts and Nevis became independent on 19 September 1983.

Betty and I were in St Kitts for a week in August that year. We heard schoolchildren practising their singing for the Independence Day celebrations. It was the last time we saw Rufus. He was living in the house at 39 Cayon Street, where his younger brother Harry had lived, next door to Greenways. By then, he had been back home for nine years and had buried not only Harry but also his sister Howard.

In those nine years every plate of his dinner service had been broken either in accidents or in fits of temper. Not one survived intact. But he had the pieces and used the larger ones for main courses and the smaller ones for puddings or for toast or bread and butter.

And he had a small cat, which he pretended to dislike but secretly loved. He had rescued it one rainy night when it was a kitten and he heard it crying in the garden at Greenways. He called it 'That damned cat' and was very pleased when Betty de-fleaed it for him.

There was also a small frog, who lived in his kitchen sink and could not be disturbed. No washing up could be done until Mr Frog had vacated the sink.

In addition there were a number of young men who visited him and performed various services for him. One of them, Edward Ryan, often slept at the house and kept an eye on Rufus.

In July 1986 George Walker wrote to me, saying that Rufus had been in a very bad state four or five weeks previously but there had been a very great improvement and he was "talking rationally and not shouting and swearing all the time". By April the next year, he was in hospital with cancer of the rectum. I prepared to fly out but he cabled me "PLEASE POSTPONE VISIT UNTIL I CAN ENJOY IT LOVE RUFUS". On 12 June 1987 he died.

The funeral (for some reason the corpse was wearing evening dress) was at St George's with the Archdeacon presiding; the burial at Springfield Cemetery with George Walker, the previous Archdeacon, doing the committal. The Governor General wife's attended in a personal capacity, but not a single member of Dr Simmonds' government was there. The previous Governor, Sir Probyn Inniss, was one of the bearers. *The Labour Spokesman* took the unusual step of printing Canon Walker's address in place of its usual editorial.

"Throughout his life", George said, "he had a great propensity for making friends with all kinds of people and almost as great a propensity for quarrelling with them; few of his friends have not felt the lash of his tongue at one time or another, but the generosity of his nature soon healed broken friendships....His last years have been spent in his native land. Sadly his great hope of establishing a national museum was not realised in his lifetime but, when such is established, it is to be hoped that his name will be honoured as its progenitor....

"He has been a valuable catalyst in our society. His never very certain temper has often exasperated his friends but never destroyed their friendship. One may speculate that her nuns often found the Prioress in Chaucer's *Canterbury Tales* difficult and even exasperating but on her beads there hung a brooch 'on which there was first write a crowned A and after *Amor vincit omnia*'. Let that be our last thought of Rufus: 'Love conquers all things'."

Chapter 6

Howard, Milly and Harry

A cheerfully deaf aunt and an uncle
profoundly affected
by the second world war

In a small plot at Springfield Cemetery in Basseterre there are three small, simple gravestones. I put up two of them in 1987. One bears the names of my King grandparents and their dates; the other the names of Rufus and of his siblings, Howard and Harry. Between these two stones is a much older stone with the name EMILY DE KLEIST KING, the dates Aug 3 1910 and Apr 18 1916 and the words 'Is it well with the child? It is well'.

Sadly, I know nothing about this little girl, my grandparents' fourth child, who died aged five, except that my mother felt her death very deeply. I have no idea why she was called de Kleist or why she died so young.

Milly came two years after Howard, who was born on Hallowe'en 1908, and 11 years before Harry. Most of the Howards I know are men but this one was a woman. She was given her mother's first name, Lilian, and her father's middle name, Howard, and, presumably to avoid confusion with her mother, was always called Howard. She trained as a nurse in London but was profoundly deaf, and this made a nursing career impossible. Despite her handicap, she was amazingly cheerful; she never made a fuss or complained about her deafness.

Howard's birthday parties tended to be fancy dress affairs with witches, broomsticks and pumpkins. She used to send me, when I was an adult and she was middle-aged, long, detailed lists of her birthday presents. She lived at home with her parents while they were still alive, and subsequently with a widowed friend, Evelyn Gibson. Howard died in April 1975, some seven months after Rufus had returned home.

Harry was the last of the King babies, arriving 11 years after Milly and 16 years after my mother, in 1921. He was christened Henry Maitland. Henry was his grandfather's name; I don't know where the Maitland came from.

Rufus arranged, and probably paid, for him to go to school in England: a minor public school in Hertfordshire called Aldenham and founded in 1597. He completed his schooling in July 1939 but was still in England when war broke out in September. Rufus put him and his widowed aunt, Mrs Thurston, on a ship going to New York. They escaped the U-boats but had a nasty encounter with a hurricane which led to his aunt being hospitalised in New York. Harry eventually reached St Kitts, but by February 1941 he was a trooper in the Duke of York's Royal Canadian Hussars. He was 19 and raring to go.

After three months he was complaining that he had been taught to scrub, wash, dust and polish but not how to handle a Bren gun or to drive a carrier. It seems that he was in a special unit of 'A' Squadron of the 3rd Canadian Division. I am not sure when they were sent to England, perhaps in 1941 or 1942.

Battle of Arnhem

He must have eventually been taught to use a Bren gun and drive a carrier as that is what he did during his active service. He took part, I believe, in the battle of Arnhem and Nijmegen in September 1944, an air-borne operation that aimed to secure a bridgehead over the River Rhine for an Allied drive to the heart of Germany. It failed, with 7,600 casualities.

Harry spent eight icy weeks of the last winter of the war in Waal, a small hamlet on the south bank of the Rhine. The Germans held the north bank, and Harry was never sure whether the creaking of the ice on the river during the night was caused by nature or by prowling Germans. In May 1945 he helped liberate the Netherlands, and shortly afterwards found his half-starving cousin Olaf Heyligers and presented him with a knapsack of biscuits, Spam and other goodies.

After the war Harry was discharged from the Canadian army in Montreal and returned to St Kitts in March 1946. But the Canadian government was ready to pay for the further education of ex-servicemen whose education had been interrupted by the war. So he went back to Canada and did a degree at the University of British Columbia.

According to Philip Larkin, 'They fuck you up, your mum and dad'. Harry was fucked up by his mum and dad, and by the war, and by Rufus. His mother was incapable of showing affection. His father, a most interesting man, always had to be the centre of attention. He used to say: "When I speak, let no dog bark!". Harry felt unloved, lonely, misunderstood and undervalued.

The war had a profound effect on him. According to his notebook, "bombs, shells, mortar bombs, aeroplane machine guns, other machine-gun bullets, land mines etc exploded almost on top of me, almost under me, just over my head, between my legs and so on. Among others my two best friends were killed just near me, one on 19 October 1944 at Watervilet in Belgium, the other on 8 May 1945 near to Leer in Germany 20 minutes before the war ended".

He was also affected by the deaths of his two best childhood friends. His cousin Lynn Walwyn, at school with Harry in England, died suddenly of a brain tumour in 1938, aged 14. And Sydney Delisle was killed in Italy during the war.

Harry's relationship with Rufus was a complex but unhappy one. Rufus was 15 years older and was, undoubtedly, very clever. "He has always been brilliant", Harry wrote in his notebook, "but the poor fool has no common sense. No one would believe that GHK and LMK [Harry's parents] could produce a younger son with plenty of common sense and quite enough intelligence to do well in several fields."

Harry and Rufus were both gay. Harry had been seduced by a boy at his public school and probably had more sex than Rufus. Because of his own proclivities, Rufus was keenly interested in Harry's relationships and possibly envious of them. "Glad you and John are helping each other," the older brother wrote to the younger in 1964. "I think the first need in both cases is to find a job which is satisfying in that it makes you feel that you are contributing something to society. Then you need someone to share that contribution with you -- and not merely your bed."

And in 1966: "Of course I knew about your relationship with James. You needn't worry so much about it. I have been considering a similar one myself....I think I helped you once ... by saying that the really important thing was the nature of the relationship, not the physical details."

Rufus' letters to Harry were full of instructions, questions and recriminations about money. It seems that Harry was supposed to be managing some land belonging to Rufus at Upper Spooners and was incapable of collecting the rents, keeping accounts or even answering Rufus' questions. And Rufus found this extremely difficult to understand and accept.

When Harry first returned to St Kitts after graduating from the University of British Columbia, he taught at the grammar school, I am not sure for how long. He had nervous breakdowns in 1954, March 1963 and April 1972. His 1972 notebook shows a very disturbed mind. He was greatly preoccupied at that time with ensuring that Aunt Em's last months [she was 92 that year] were happy and believed that God was using him to this end.

He had always been obsessed with the royal family, and this is also reflected in his notebook, where he records that he joined the Canadian army on 10 February 1941 "EXACTLY 100 years after Queen Victoria was married". Something is wrong here. She was married in 1840. It is possible that Harry joined up in 1940, not 1941, but more likely that it was the 101st anniversary of the royal wedding.

He had the whole of the 1937 coronation service of King George VI on gramophone records and used to play it over and over again on the old gramophone at Sunnyside. At the time of the 1953 coronation, I had to post out to Harry all the London newspapers and magazines with photographs of the event.

He was also obsessed with cars, and his own car was a very important part of his life. When, because of a prolonged spell of ill health, he had to sell his car, he found this extraordinarily difficult.

He came to England several times after the war, on one occasion for an operation to remove a cancerous growth from his bladder.

His last visit was, I think, in 1972. He arrived in London on 1 June, and it was immediately obvious that he was very ill. He could hardly walk and, to a layman, it seemed like a bad case of Parkinson's. A few days later, he was seen by a Dr Clein and admitted to Long Grove Hospital, near Epsom. A week later he was transferred to the National Hospital for Nervous Diseases in Queen Square. I don't know what the diagnosis was or how long he stayed in hospital, but by August he was visiting his Kittitian friends in Birmingham.

On 21 August he returned to London, two days later he had another appointment at the National Hospital, and the following day he went to Cambridge to stay with Rufus. That visit was disastrous. He and Rufus had a violent argument, and three days later Harry was brought back to London by the Dean of the Pembroke and handed over to Betty and myself.

We took him home, where, the next day, he attempted to kill himself by slashing his wrists in our bathroom. He was then readmitted to Long Grove Hospital. Betty and I, my mother and my sister, and Rufus visited him a number of times and within three weeks he seemed much better. Three and a half weeks later he was discharged, but five days later he was back inside. Poor Harry! I have no record of when he returned to St Kitts but it must have been before the end of the year.

Harry had been unemployed from July 1964 to January 1969 and then got a job with Higgs and Hill, the construction firm, as personnel officer. I don't know how long that lasted. Later on, or it may have been earlier, I am not sure, he worked for the government as St Kitts' very first community welfare officer.

In that job Harry believed that he was fulfilling a family tradition. "Generosity," he said, "is the family failing or weakness of the Kings and the Burts, and our forbears, who are now cursed by some of our local politicians, did their duty nobly to the poor."

Harry died with much pain (cancer of the stomach) in July 1975, aged only 53. His friend Arthur Leaman says he was very stoic. Rufus started a fund dedicated to the memory of the the island's first community welfare officer and charged with continuing the charitable work that Harry and Canon Walker had carried out for so many years.

Chapter 7

Granny and Brampa

The local historian and patriot, the wife
with thoughts too deep for smiles or tears,
some earlier King ancestors, and the Savery family

My mother's mother, christened Lilian Mary, did not leave a strong impression on my memory. She was tall and very thin, did not smile easily and found it difficult to show affection. In a letter to Rufus, his father wrote: "Both your parents have a way of suppressing their feelings that may make them seem unfeeling. This is most true of your mother whose thoughts are fequently too deep for either smiles or tears. Her upbringing in a hard household may have had much to do with developing this."

She presided over the housekeeping arrangements at Sunnyside and had a cook to do the cooking (on coal-pots) and a maid to clean and wait at table. The mahogany furniture in her small drawing room, looking out onto Warner Park, gleamed, and the silver shone.

I don't think she had much education. She came to England twice, possibly three times, most memorably in 1938 when we took over the annexe to a hotel in Seaview, Isle of Wight, and filled it with at least nine members of my mother's West Indian family plus my father's sister, Con. Lilian Mary Burt was born in November 1882 and died at Sunnyside in February 1958, aged 75.

I know much more about my maternal grandfather, whom I called Brampa. George Howard King was born in St Kitts in 1871, and began work in a lawyer's office when he was 18. A year later he entered the local civil service, as an acting revenue officer. He worked successively in the Commissioner's office, the Registrar's office, the magistrates' courts and the Treasury before being given a permanent appointment as a clerk in the Post Office in St Kitts in 1895.

Three years later he was Revenue Officer, Nevis, then Government Officer for the Northern District, St Kitts, then back to his old job in Nevis in 1905, the year my mother was born. The following year he was made 1st Clerk in the Post Office in St Kitts and Sub Inspector of Schools. Then nine years later he became Postmaster of St Kitts, the post he held from 1915 until his retirement at the end of 1935. As Postmaster he earned £350 a year plus £58 'personal', whatever that meant.

In 1936 he was a member of the island's Legislative Council. He was made a Companion of the Imperial Service Order (For Faithful Service) on King George V's birthday, 3 June 1932. I have the letter from Government House telling my grandfather that it had given His Majesty much pleasure to confer upon him the dignity of Companionship of the Order, and that it would be announced at the king's birthday parade that morning.

Dining at Government House subsequently, Brampa dropped his medal in the soup, fished it out, licked it clean and pinned it back on his dinner jacket.

But it was as chairman of the Historic Sites and Records Committee and as chairman of the Warner Park Committee that he made major contributions to his island home.

In January 1922 Brampa wrote to His Honour the Administrator pointing out that 28 January 1923 would be the 300th anniversary of the island's colonisation. In fact it was on 28 January 1624 that Thomas Warner, a captain in the bodyguard of King James I, had arrived in Old Road Bay, St Kitts, with 14 other settlers. It seems that my grandfather and the authorities were unaware or forgot that until 1752 the Julian calendar was in use in England and that the year started on 25 March. So that 28 January 1623 Old Style was 28 January 1624 in the (New Style) Gregorian calendar.

Anyhow, Brampa argued that it would be fitting that there should be a tercentenary celebration and suggested that a postage stamp of suitable design should be issued with the money raised from its sale devoted to a public purpose that would stand as a permanent record of the tercentenary.

He further suggested that the Losack lands might be purchased and made into a park and recreation ground. "By this conversion of the Losack fields, that which is now a menace, if not an actual danger to the health of the town, would become a means of promoting its healthfulness."

The sum of £3,916 was raised from the sale of the tercentenary stamps, and the government bought the 14 acres of land, still under cultivation with sugar cane, for £1,400. The rest of the money raised was used for levelling the site and building a pavilion. And on 5 January 1928 Warner Park, named in honour of the founder of the Mother Colony of the English and French Antilles, was officially opened by the administrator, Colonel Reginald St Johnston.

My grandparents' home, Sunnyside, in Lozac Road, looked out over Warner Park.

St Kitts is in debt to my grandfather not only for Warner Park but also for his tireless work over very many years for the preservation and restoration of Brimstone Hill. As he himself wrote: "Brimstone Hill -- the Gibraltar of the West Indies -- is *the* historic spot of an historic island. In the poverty of the present it deserves to live on the memory of the past, for the part it once played in the history of the British Empire is none the less worthy because unrecognised."

In 1782, when France attacked St Kitts with a strong force of 8,000 soldiers and 31 warships, there was a gallant defence of the Brimstone Hill fortress for more than a month by a garrison which had been heavily outnumbered and outgunned from the start, while Rodney was coming across the Atlantic to meet and defeat de Grasse in the Empire-saving Battle of the Saints.

The fortress was abandoned as a place of defence in 1853, and for 50 years no one took any interest in the place. The cannon were removed, and there was much vandalism. Then, at the turn of the century, the government started to allocate an annual sum for clearing brush and maintaining the remaining buildings.

By 1930 about 30 cannon had been replaced at the citadel and the Prince of Wales Bastion. The fortress was then being looked after by an organisation known as the Historic Sites and Records Committee, with my grandfather as one of its most active and enthusiatic members. D L Matheson CBE in *The Brimstone Hill Fortress*, published in 1986, says: "The work of the Historic Sites Committee continued until early in the 1960s, and the importance of their contribution should never be underestimated".

Like his English counterpart, my West Indian grandfather was a prolific writer, but while the former wrote about religion, Brampa wrote about history and, in particular, about the history of St Kitts. His pamphlet about Brimstone Hill, *The Gibraltar of the West Indies: A Chapter from British Imperial History*, was first published in, I think, 1929. It was published in the 1930s by the West India Committee in London and in the 1960s by the National Geographic Society. It ran to at least eight editions.

After Rufus died in 1987, I was moved to discover that back in 1929 he had had a copy of the pamphlet specially bound in hard covers and inscribed "The Author from his son (Pembroke College, Cambridge 1929)". There was also a little poem that Rufus had written:

> These covers twain enshrine a story
> Of stiring deeds and ancient glory
> Writ by one who loved full well
> The Epic of his Isle to tell.
>
> Thou, little book, set'st forth his name
> Whose pride was all his Island's fame
> Who round her name a glamour cast
> Recalling oft her honoured past.
>
> In manner then as best befits
> The proud Historian of St Kitts
> Preserve for all Posterity
> Her record, and his memory!

And my grandfather responded as follows:

Though small is the part I've played in Life's game,
No riches are mine, nor prowess, nor fame,
Content should I be with things as they are
While through a dark sky my Son is my Star.

A less substantial pamphlet was *Historic St Christopher: Scenes and Memories Along the Road*. And he wrote a regular, or it may have been irregular, column in *The St Kitts-Nevis Daily Bulletin* in return for a free copy of the paper. I have the cuttings of many of Brampa's articles that appeared in the 1940s and which he posted to me in Trinidad, Barbados and England. Their titles include 'Lawyer Stephen's Cave', 'The McMahon Library & the Poore Memorial School', 'Fig Tree Fort', 'Breda', 'Military Tombs in St Kitts', 'Our Silver Mine', 'What Mean .... These Stones', 'The Guns That Travelled', 'The Circus', 'Middle Island Churchyard', and many, many more.

I do not know what sort of education he had, presumably in St Kitts or possibly Antigua, but he knew a lot of history and was very well read.

I remember him well. He always, or almost always, wore white cotton drill trousers and a white cotton drill tunic with a mandarin collar with little underneath: jock-strap like underpants, possibly a vest, but no shirt. And he usually wore an dirty old grey trilby with a hole cut in the crown. This was so that, when his hat blew off, he could pick it up with a hook that he had fixed to the handle of his riding whip.

As Harry recorded in his notebook, Brampa was "a most interesting man .... full of jokes and interesting stories". He helped me build a chicken-run for some chickens I was keeping at Rozelle and, when I left St Kitts for Trinidad in 1939, I gave him my black and white mongrel Pip.

He used to train race horses, and there were many silver cups from races won in the drawing-room at Sunnyside. I can remember, as a small boy, helping to feed two or three horses in his stables, but I think that only one of them belonged to him. But I may be wrong. I used to go riding with him and certainly assumed at the time that both the horses were his.

He built himself a two-wheeled pony trap with bicycle wheels and pneumatic tyres, a unique contraption but it took him from Basseterre to Upper Spooners and back with comfort and efficiency. It had been his ambition to own three acres and a cow up in the mountains, and Upper Spooners was the realisation of his dream, although it was rather more than three acres, and there was no cow. He built a small house there, as cheaply as possible. Probably too cheaply, as it blew down a few years later.

My grandfather was a Christian but didn't go to church. He believed that he could worship God more effectively in the open air at Upper Spooners than at St George's church.

The view from his little house up there was possibly the best in the world. On the one side you looked over Cayon Village, Lodge Estate and Nicola Town to the blue sea with St Barts and St Maarten on the horizon. On the other you could see the undulating Conaree Hills, Frigate Bay, Salt Ponds, Nevis and more blue sea. His little house in the hills gave my grandfather enormous pleasure in the final years of his life.

He died on 19 October 1951, aged 80, and was buried next to his little daughter, Milly, in Springfield Cemetery.

My grandfather's brothers and sisters

Brampa had four sisters and three brothers, and I know next to nothing about six of the seven. The eldest of his siblings was Emily Verplank King, who was born in 1857. As far as I know, she never married. Brampa's three brothers, Edmund, Bryan and Henry certainly remained unmarried. Child number 4, Annie Earle, married Alan Otty Thurston, who had been manager of Canada Estate for very many years and attorney for the Wade family in Dominica, Montserrat and Nevis as well as in St Kitts. He died in 1933, aged 80, when I was five, so I don't remember him. But I remember his widow well.

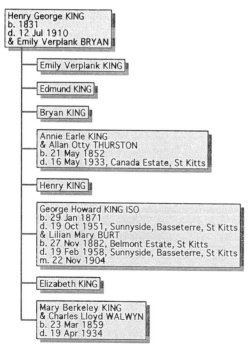

Henry George KING
b. 1831
d. 12 Jul 1910
& Emily Verplank BRYAN

Emily Verplank KING

Edmund KING

Bryan KING

Annie Earle KING
& Allan Otty THURSTON
b. 21 May 1852
d. 16 May 1933, Canada Estate, St Kitts

Henry KING

George Howard KING ISO
b. 29 Jan 1871
d. 19 Oct 1951, Sunnyside, Basseterre, St Kitts
& Lilian Mary BURT
b. 27 Nov 1882, Belmont Estate, St Kitts
d. 19 Feb 1958, Sunnyside, Basseterre, St Kitts
m. 22 Nov 1904

Elizabeth KING

Mary Berkeley KING
& Charles Lloyd WALWYN
b. 23 Mar 1859
d. 19 Apr 1934

For some reason, we all knew her as Miss Annie. After her husband's death, she left Canada Estate and build a house called Lilac Cottage opposite the Moravian Chapel at the corner of Victoria Road and Taylor's Range. It was perhaps a ten minute walk to Sunnyside.

Miss Annie always wore black, and I can remember, as a child at Sunnyside, seeing this black dot appear in the distance and gradually get larger and larger as she walked across Warner Park to tell me a bedtime story.

In 1939, returning from England on the outbreak of war, she suffered serious injuries when her ship encountered a hurricane and the grand piano, sliding across the sloping ballroom floor, crashed into her. She was hospitalised in New York and died some weeks later.

My grandfather was the sixth child and had two younger sisters: Elizabeth who married someone in Canada, and Mary Berekeley who married Charles Lloyd Walwyn, grandfather of my second cousin Chris Walwyn, who was joint executor with me of Rufus' will.

Earlier Kings

My grandfather's father was Henry George King, born in 1831 almost certainly in St Kitts as *his* father is shown in the Saint Christopher Triennial Return of Slaves for that year as having five slaves. Henry George King was Cashier and Accountant of the St Kitts Savings Bank in 1890 and later Treasurer of St Kitts. He married Emily Verplank Bryan and died in 1910, aged 78.

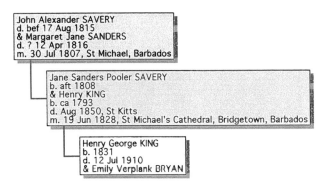

```
John Alexander SAVERY
d. bef 17 Aug 1815
& Margaret Jane SANDERS
d. ? 12 Apr 1816
m. 30 Jul 1807, St Michael, Barbados

        Jane Sanders Pooler SAVERY
        b. aft 1808
        & Henry KING
        b. ca 1793
        d. Aug 1850, St Kitts
        m. 19 Jun 1828, St Michael's Cathedral, Bridgetown, Barbados

                Henry George KING
                b. 1831
                d. 12 Jul 1910
                & Emily Verplank BRYAN
```

His slave-owning father, plain Henry King without the George, came to St Kitts from Barbados, where he had been an Ensign in the 3rd West Indian Regiment. I have found in the Public Record Office at Kew the letters he wrote seeking to dispose of his half-pay commission because of "the inadequacy of the Half Pay to the many expenses necessarily attendant on a Family and the little prospect of advancing in His Majesty's Service without the means of purchasing promotion".

He succeeded in extricating himself from his regiment and on 19 June 1828, in the cathedral in Bridgetown, married Jane Sanders Pooler Savery, the only daughter of John Alexander Savery. She was probably no more than 17 or 18 when she was married, and her groom must have been a good 15 years her senior. Henry took his young bride to St Kitts. *Howe's Almanac* for 1837 shows him as a Customs Officer-Comptroller, Landing Surveyor and Admeasurer of Vessels. He died in 1850, aged 57.

I don't really know anything about my great-great-great-grandfather King, but he was probably born in England. My grandfather told me, and I am sure he wrote the verse himself,

> My ancestor King
> Did a risky thing
> He stole a sheep
> Which he couldn't eat
> Nor yet could keep
> So when the Fleet
> Sailed over the seas
> To the Caribbees
> With cargoes of rogues
> And desperadoes
> They shipped him to Barbados.

He may well have been in Barbados and, according to a rather ambiguous letter from Rufus, he may have been in Guadeloupe 'when captured in 1794'. Unfortunately it is not clear whether Rufus was referring to the capture of my ancestor or of Guadeloupe -- or of both.

Guadeloupe was certainly captured by the British in April 1794 but by December that year the French had retaken the island, and it is at least possible that they had also taken my great-great-great-grandfather. I don't suppose I will ever know.

The Savery family

As we have seen, Henry King's father-in-law was John Alexander Savery, and the will of his grandfather, John Savery the elder, made in Barbados in July 1804, makes interesting reading. He leaves his daughter Mary Ann Thomas 'two negro girls to wit Nanny and Clarissa together with their issue and increase hereafter to be born'. One grandson gets 'a negro man named Nickey' and another grandson gets 'a negro boy mamed Toney'. And that left a further dozen slaves to be sold together with eighteen acres, one rood and five perches of land.

When I was at school, a very long time ago, five and a half yards equalled one pole, rod or perch; four poles equalled one chain; ten chains equalled one furlong; and eight furlongs equalled one mile. Back in 1804, eighteen acres,

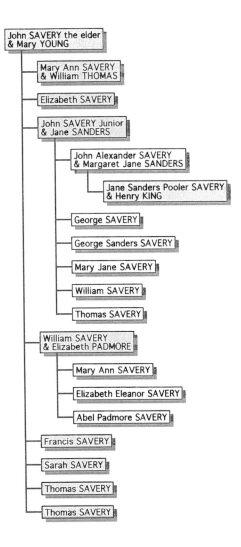

one rood and five perches of land plus more than a dozen slaves must have equalled a lot of money for my ancestors and a lot of misery for the human beings they regarded as their property and bought, sold and bequeathed.

It seems that my 4 x great-grandfather John Savery Junior was the black sheep of the family. His father, John Savery the elder, a very rich man, left him only a token £5 in his will.

And the will made it quite clear that not a penny of the income provided for John Savery Junior's wife Jane should be used to pay his debts.

The black sheep's son, John Alexander Savery, made a will in December 1808, before his daughter, Jane Sanders Pooler Savery, was born. He was 'intending shortly to depart this Island for Savannah in the United States of America'. Less than seven years later he was dead, whether in Savannah or in Barbados I know not.

He only had the one daughter, but where was she born? Did he leave his beloved wife Margaret Jane in Barbados, or did he take her with him to Georgia? Was my great-great-grandmother an American?

She was certainly in Barbados in 1828 when she married Henry King in St Michael's Cathedral in Bridgetown. The ceremony was conducted by the Revd R F King (no relation).

Chapter 8

The Burt branch of the family

*The family tree going back to 1686
found in an old tin trunk,
the Canadian Burts
and the Australian Burts*

My maternal grandmother was a Burt, and it is her branch of the family that I can trace further back into the past than any of the other branches. This is largely due to the fact that, when Rufus died in 1987, I found in an old tin trunk a family tree of about 200 names going back to Colonel William Burt, who had been Deputy Governor of Nevis and had died in 1686.

But let us start with my grandmother and work backwards. Lilian Mary Burt had six sisters and three brothers, and she was the eighth child. Her eldest sister, Alice Louisa, was born in 1870 and lived until 1954, so I knew her when I was growing up in St Kitts. She was very old and very large and always wore black; my sister and I called her Aunty.

She gave me my first (and only) Prayer Book (with hymns ancient and modern) and inscribed it 'Christopher Birch, Easter Sunday, 12th April 1936'. She was then 65 and I was almost eight.

As a young woman, she had run a hotel or boarding house in Basseterre, but that was before I knew her. When I was a child, she lived with her sister Emily in a house in Cayon Street, conveniently for her almost next door to St George's Church. Aunt Em was the librarian at the public library above the Court House in Pall Mall Square. It was there that she introduced me in December 1938 to Mrs Churchill, who was the guest of Lord Moyne on his steam yacht *Rosaura*, together with members of the Royal Commission appointed to inquire into social conditions in the British West Indies.

I don't think Aunty ever crossed the Atlantic, but Aunt Em visited Europe once. In a letter to her great-great-nephew, my son Frank, she said: "I loved the winter the year I was in England and was never too cold tho' the boarding house blankets were very thin. Crossed the North Sea (from Denmark) in Feb and loved the biting wind. But now my old bones would not take it".

Aunt Em was ten years younger than Aunty and lived on for 20 years after Aunty's death, dying, aged 93, just seven weeks before I took my wife out to St Kitts for the first time. That was a great pity as I would have liked Betty to meet her.

Aunt Em had the Burt nose. When I met Sir Francis Burt for the first time, he reminded me strongly of her. She once rashly asked my sister what she

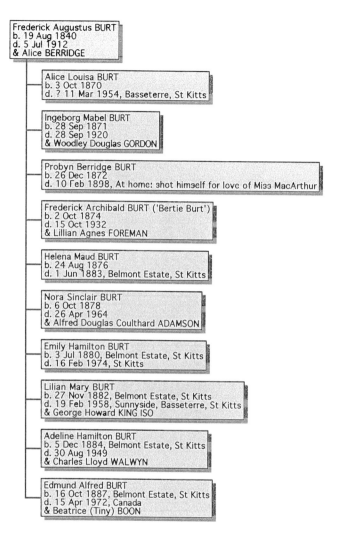

Frederick Augustus BURT
b. 19 Aug 1840
d. 5 Jul 1912
& Alice BERRIDGE

Alice Louisa BURT
b. 3 Oct 1870
d. ? 11 Mar 1954, Basseterre, St Kitts

Ingeborg Mabel BURT
b. 28 Sep 1871
d. 28 Sep 1920
& Woodley Douglas GORDON

Probyn Berridge BURT
b. 26 Dec 1872
d. 10 Feb 1898, At home: shot himself for love of Miss MacArthur

Frederick Archibald BURT ('Bertie Burt')
b. 2 Oct 1874
d. 15 Oct 1932
& Lillian Agnes FOREMAN

Helena Maud BURT
b. 24 Aug 1876
d. 1 Jun 1883, Belmont Estate, St Kitts

Nora Sinclair BURT
b. 6 Oct 1878
d. 26 Apr 1964
& Alfred Douglas Coulthard ADAMSON

Emily Hamilton BURT
b. 3 Jul 1880, Belmont Estate, St Kitts
d. 16 Feb 1974, St Kitts

Lilian Mary BURT
b. 27 Nov 1882, Belmont Estate, St Kitts
d. 19 Feb 1958, Sunnyside, Basseterre, St Kitts
& George Howard KING ISO

Adeline Hamilton BURT
b. 5 Dec 1884, Belmont Estate, St Kitts
d. 30 Aug 1949
& Charles Lloyd WALWYN

Edmund Alfred BURT
b. 16 Oct 1887, Belmont Estate, St Kitts
d. 15 Apr 1972, Canada
& Beatrice (Tiny) BOON

would do if she had a nose like hers, only to receive the reply: "Fish with it!".
The Burt nose was also carried by three of the Canadian Burts: Ivor, Daphne
and Donald.

Aunty and Aunt Em were the only two of my grandmother's sisters that I
knew at all well. Aunt Nora (Nora Sinclair Burt, 1878-1964) and Aunt Addie
(Adeline Hamilton Burt, 1884-1949) I knew slightly, the other great-aunts and
the three great-uncles I knew not at all.

My grandmother's parents' second child was Ingeborg Mabel Burt, who died in 1920, eight years before I was born. I knew her daughter Vi and Vi's two sons, Earle and Bruce. Earle had psychiatric problems; Bruce stopped a bullet in the war which paralysed him from the waist down. He married Berkeley Walwyn.

The third child and first son was Probyn Berridge Burt. He committed suicide in 1898, aged 25, 'for the love of a Miss MacArthur'. He had fallen in love with this young lady, and it is not clear to what extent his feelings were reciprocated.

But the Fleet was in, it seemed that Miss MacArthur got involved with a naval officer, and young Probyn promptly shot himself.

The next child was Frederick Archibald Burt, known, I am not sure why, as 'Bertie Burt', pronounced Butty Butt. He was born in 1874 and died when I was four, so I don't remember him.

But I knew his widow, Agnes, and his son and daughter, Leonard and Aimee. Bertie Burt was a sugar planter. Aimee says: "One of my best memories of Daddy was the many times he'd take me with him when he went down to the estates -- Pump, La Vallee and Cranstoun's. I'd really enjoy that -- often playing with the overseer's children while he inspected everything, riding around the estate. And all the 'goodies' we'd often bring home: coconuts, cane etc. Also, every night before dinner, he'd mix a weak, very sweet rum cocktail and, any time I wanted, he'd let me have a small sip! He was good natured and kind".

His wife, Lillian Agnes Foreman, was a Roman Catholic, and he left the Church of England and became a Catholic himself. Their children were, of course, brought up as Roman Catholics. Leonard, who did a lot to keep the Burt family tree up to date, was murdered in St Croix in 1973. Aimee is living, aged 82, in Kansas, USA, while I write this.

Not only was Aimee's brother murdered, her husband, Arvid Johnson, was killed, aged 41, when his plane crashed into the Caribbean Sea, and their younger son, Steven, broke his neck in a car accident in 2001 and was paralysed from the neck down.

The next of my grandmother's siblings was Helena Maud, who died in 1883, aged six. She was followed by Aunt Nora, who married Alfred Adamson, an engineer and sugar estate manager in St Kitts and Colombia. They had two daughters, Marguerite and Bea. Bea was one of my mother's closest friends. She married Fabian Camacho, a magistrate and later a judge in Trinidad.

Fabian found it difficult to sit still and always sat in a rocking chair in court, rocking backwards and forwards as he listened to the evidence and gave judgment.

A famous Trinidadian criminal sentenced to death by Fabian, after his third trial for murder, was Boysie Singh. Fabian's grandson, Anthony Milne, wrote the following poem about Boysie.

HOW I BORN AND GROW

I, John Boysie Singh,
Born April 5, 1908,
At 17 Luis Street, Woodbrook,
Port of Spain,
Son of Bhagrang Singh from Punjab,
A Chutri warrior,
Formerly Indian Army.
He had a fine steel sword
With a hawk-head handle
And rubies eyes
That he pray over once every year.
He work as night watchman
On sugar estate,
Whilst Ma travel in the country
Selling cloth.
Last one of four children,
Eldest brother 28 years older,
Sister 14 years,
And a next sister four years
When I born.
I attend at Ackal's and
Newtown Boys RC,
A "intractable pupil"
They call me,
And I try to learn three Rs
And fight.
In 1919, when 11,
They arrest me for flying kite,
With zwill and pulling mange
They say,
At Woodbrook Savannah and
Hold me overnight in cell,
Give six strokes with a tamarind rod,
Till I piss my pants,
But I didn't bawl.
This make me a badjohn.
I catch blue crab
Near Hot-and-Cold
and thief some,
Lime and pitch marble and
Gamble with sebby-lebby
Under a tree at Wrightson Road,
And fight a big man called Harris.
Then went to sea with Black Joe
For rowing race and
Bets on this.
I jostle boats
Then fish in the Gulf and
Swim out alone to ships
In the stream.
That is how I born and
Grow to love the sea,
And everything in it.

Fabian and Bea had three daughters and a son. Their eldest daughter,
Patricia, married James Errol Malcolm Milne, and it was their son, Anthony, a
journalist, who wrote the above poem.

Aunt Em, already mentioned, came next and was followed two years later by my grandmother. Another two-year gap and Aunt Addie was born. She married in 1908 Charles Lloyd Walwyn as his second wife. Lloyd Walwyn's first wife was my grandfather's youngest sister, Mary Berkeley King. So I am doubly related to the Walwyns.

Aunt Addie had five children, but I only knew the youngest two, Daphne and Douglas. Daphne asked me to be godfather to her younger son, Timothy, and I gave him a silver christening mug with his name on it. Douglas read law after the war and became a magistrate in Jamaica, where he died.

The Canadian Burts
Edmund Alfred Burt was the youngest of my grandmother's brothers and was born in St Kitts. When he left school, his father, who owned a sugar estate, gave him a job as overseer of the rum still. But his prospects did not look good and, in 1887 when he was 18, he emigrated to Canada and worked for the first two years as a cowboy on a large cattle ranch near Calgary.

What a contrast with St Kitts that must have been, with temperatures often plunging to minus 40 degrees Fahrenheit (which, interestingly, is the same as minus 40 degrees Celsius) and the bitter north wind unimpeded by any mountains.

In fact his first winter was relatively mild but his second winter was just too cold and the following year, after seeing an advertisement saying "Come to Kamloops where you can work in your shirtsleeves all winter", he decided to give it a try.

He ran into Oliver and Alfred Boon, with whom he had been at school in St Kitts and who were working at a sawmill in Kamloops. Edmund got a job at the same mill, and the three of them lived in tents by the river, cooking their meals over campfires.

Edmund soon found a homestead south east of Ussher Lake and erected a small log cabin. He then married Beatrice (Tiny) Boon, Oliver's and Alfred's sister, who had also been born in St Kitts, and they had eight children.

Four of them are still alive, and there are many grandchildren and great grandchildren. Edmund Alfred Burt's descendants, dead and alive,constitute the Canadian Burts. I have 88 of them on my family tree.

They are outnumbered by the Australian Burts, who also originated in St Kitts, and who run to well over 200.

Edmund's eldest son Les and his second son Ivor were in the same brigade of the 3rd Canadian Division as my Uncle Harry during the second world war so they saw quite a lot of each other. After the war, when Harry was studying at the University of British Columbia, he spent some of his vacations at the Burt ranch at Monte Lake.

The Canadian Burts are now spread across Canada from Ontario in the East, where Edmund's daughter Nora lives, to British Columbia in the West, where

Edmund Alfred BURT
b. 16 Oct 1887, Belmont Estate, St Kitts
d. 15 Apr 1972, Canada
& Beatrice (Tiny) BOON
b. 8 Oct 1893, Basseterre, St Kitts
d. 4 Nov 1988, Shuswap Lake General Hospital, British Columbia, Canada
m. 6 Jul 1911

Edmund Leslie BURT
b. 9 Jun 1912
d. 18 Apr 1992, Canada
& Sally Walrond BICKFORD
b. 8 Apr 1934, Looe, Cornwall
m. 27 Sep 1958, Looe, Cornwall

Alice Emily (Babs) BURT
b. 15 Feb 1914
d. 5 Sep 2002
& Frederick William HOBBINS
b. 31 Jul 1908
d. 4 Sep 1985
m. 1 Mar 1937

Frederick Ivor BURT
b. 16 Jun 1916
d. 17 Oct 2002, Queensland, Australia
& Phyllis Dorothy WHITEFIELD
b. 2 May 1923, New Zealand
m. 5 Jun 1948, Vancouver

Henry Hamilton BURT
b. 12 Aug 1918
d. 31 Jul 2000
& Margaret LAMBERT
b. 23 Jul 1924
m. 1 Jun 1946

Nora Pearl BURT
b. 8 Feb 1922
& Harry Evered GRIMMON
b. 19 May 1923
d. 13 Jul 1966
m. 8 Mar 1946

Nora Pearl BURT
b. 8 Feb 1922
& Harold Edmund BARTMAN
b. 11 Nov 1929
m. 10 Oct 1969

Daphne Elaine BURT
b. 10 Sep 1925
& Charles Dermot GROVE-WHITE
b. 13 Nov 1918
d. 9 Dec 1998, British Columbia
m. 12 Aug 1950

Ronald Walter BURT
b. 20 Feb 1927
& Gloria Daphne ATKINSON
b. 28 Mar 1925, New Zealand
m. 25 Feb 1950

Donald Irving BURT
b. 26 Jan 1929
& Jean Doris CLARKE
b. 15 Apr 1929, Blackpool, England
m. 30 Apr 1955

his daughter-in-law Sally and his daughter Daphne both have their homes.

Fred and Alice
My grandmother's parents were Frederick Augustus Burt and Alice Berridge. They were married in 1868, and just three years later they inherited the four children of Frederick's older brother Archibald and his wife Laura, who both died within four days of each other in Grenada, where Archibald was Attorney-General.

The eldest of the four orphans was seven, the youngest two. And Frederick and Alice already had two children of their own and were to have eight more. When they were first married, my great-grandparents lived at Caines Estate, some 16 miles from Basseterre. Aunt Em says that her mother: "found life very lonely. She came from a large family and was always gay at home, but my father did not approve of too much gaiety and was quite satisfied to let his work absorb him and did not think it fitting for a poor manager's wife to go to balls when ships were in".

The work that absorbed Frederick Augustus Burt was managing 578 acres of sugar cane at Caines, then 512 acres at Willett's and eventually 844 at Belmont. His photograph, hanging in my living room, shows a heavily bearded good-looking gentleman wearing a waitcoat, a cravat and a stern expression. His wife, with her hair up, is leaning on a chair and wearing an elaborate dress with a bustle.

Frederick and Alice looked after the four orphans for six years until their grandfather, who had emigrated to Australia, arranged for them to be shipped via London to Perth, where they were cared for by their Uncle Septimus.

Aunt Em's story continues: "We jogged along at Belmont, always very poor and always someone else's children for my mother to look after, tho' she had her hands full with her own.... After the Burt children went away, one of my aunts who had married a Dane in St Croix, Dr Kalmer, died. When news of her illness came, my mother and her father left in a sailing vessel for St Croix, but she had died and the funeral over by the time they got there. After staying a while with the bereaved husband, my mother brought the two younger girls back to St Kitts with her, the other children, three girls and a boy, being at school in Denmark".

So up to 1878, Frederick and Alice had been looking after the four orphans and five of their own children. Then 12 years later, in 1889, they took on two more motherless children in addition to their own flock, now numbering nine, as little Maud had died in 1883. By then Aunty, their first child, was 19, and baby Edmund was only two. But Aunt Em was nine, more or less the same age as the two newcomers, and she very much enjoyed their companionship.

In fact she became very fond of them and corresponded with them long after they were married and lived in Denmark and the Netherlands. She says: "I can quite recollect all our play and the walks to pick guavas and visits to the cane heap. We were very fond of the sugar cane and would each choose several and sit in the garden. When my father found this out, we were limited to two apiece much to our disgust.

"We led a very simple life, no parties, the one great occasion once a year was the Church Bazaar held in Basseterre, when each parish would be represented -- generally held in the Court House. We would all go to town and stay at Grandfather Berridge's -- it meant two new dresses and many tips from various uncles, the only time we had anything to spend, so it was always a Red Letter Day, more so than Christmas which was very quiet."

Aunt Em's main memory of Christmas was the carol singing by the labourers on the sugar estate, each of whom received a glass of wine or grog and a bun when they had finished singing. It was the children's job to hand out the buns and they "would lie awake from early listening for 'Good morning to the Master, Good morning to the Mistress' and bound out of bed and get ready for them -- sometimes at 2.00am."

The Australian Burts

My great-grandfather was the third of Archibald Paull Burt's 12 children. The unusual spelling of that second name was that of the surname of his godfather. Archie gave his first six children two names each: George Henry, Archibald Piguenit, Frederick Augustus (he was born in August), Edward Musgrave, John Musgrave and Edmund Wigley. By the time his seventh child was born, he was getting tired of thinking up new names and his imagination was failing. The seventh was simply called Septimus, the eighth Octavius. Then a new burst of energy resulted in Alfred Earle followed by Francis Sinclair, Louisa Emily and Mina Eliza. The first 11 children were all born in St Kitts, the twelfth in Australia.

Archibald Paull Burt was sent by his father to a private school in Richmond, Surrey, and was admitted to the Middle Temple to study law at the amazingly tender age of 14. That was in 1825. In 1830, still a minor, he returned to St Kitts. And, although not formally called to the bar in England, his Middle Temple qualification was sufficient for his admission that year to the bar of St Christopher.

He built up a successful legal practice and also formed a trading partnership with another barrister, Francis Spencer Wigley. Their earnings as barristers provided them with the capital to invest in a number of sugar estates. By 1834 Archie owned three slaves: "Sarah, black, about 40, a washer; John, sambo, 12 years, a house servant; John, black, 1 year".

In 1836 Archie married Louisa Bryan, daughter of Dr John Bryan, at St George's, Basseterre. The ceremony was performed by the Revd Daniel Gateward Davis, who six years later was to become the first Bishop of Antigua.

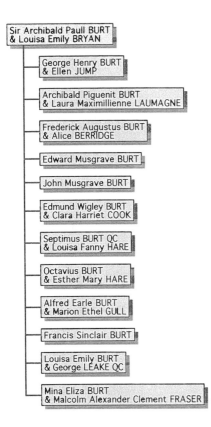

Sir Archibald Paull BURT
& Louisa Emily BRYAN

George Henry BURT
& Ellen JUMP

Archibald Piguenit BURT
& Laura Maximillienne LAUMAGNE

Frederick Augustus BURT
& Alice BERRIDGE

Edward Musgrave BURT

John Musgrave BURT

Edmund Wigley BURT
& Clara Harriet COOK

Septimus BURT QC
& Louisa Fanny HARE

Octavius BURT
& Esther Mary HARE

Alfred Earle BURT
& Marion Ethel GULL

Francis Sinclair BURT

Louisa Emily BURT
& George LEAKE QC

Mina Eliza BURT
& Malcolm Alexander Clement FRASER

In 1837, following a family tradition, Archie was commissioned as a Lieutenant-Colonel and made aide-de-camp to the Lieutenant-Governor. By 1838 he was a notary public. He became a member of the Legislative and Executive Councils and of the Administrative Committee and later followed in his father's footsteps to become Speaker of the House of Assembly. He served as Coroner for the island. A leading layman in the Church of England, he was Chancellor of the Diocese of Antigua between 1855 and 1860.

But his legal career was all important. In 1845 he had returned to England and had been called to the bar. In 1848 he was provisionally appointed Attorney-General of St Kitts and Anguilla. In 1849 the appointment was confirmed, the Lieutenant-Governor having told the Governor

Of unblemished private character Mr Burt unites many qualities which befit a servant of the Crown in the position for which I should strongly recommend him. His qualifications strictly professional are sufficiently attested by his eminent station at the Bar of this island while he is endowed with considerable power of application to business as well as with that sound common sense and equal temper that are peculiarly wanted this office.

The salary was £300 a year, half that paid to the Chief Justice. In 1856 the Chief Justice died after 'a fit of apoplexy while sitting on the Bench at Nevis', and the Lieutenant-Governor of St Kitts wrote to the Governor of the Leeward Islands in Antigua saying: "I purpose appointing provisionally Mr A P Burt" to the vacant Chief Justiceship. The Governor was outraged and vetoed the appointment, writing to Henry Labouchere, the Secretary of State for the Colonies, to say:

> You having been pleased to affirm the principle that it is not desirable that men should succeed to the Bench in the Colony in which they have practised and been long resident, I felt I could not depart from that principle by sanctioning the appointment of Mr Burt, the rule being peculiarly applicable to the existing circumstances in St Christopher.

It was now the turn of the Lieutenant-Governor to be affronted, and he wrote again, pressing for Burt's appointment and referring to his "high legal reputation and great talent, probably equal to if not greater than any Lawyer in the West Indies, and also the unbounded esteem in which he is held in this community".

More acrimonious letters were exchanged, and the Governor sought the support of the Secretary of State, knowing that it was unlikely, whatever the merits of the case, that his decision as Governor would be countermanded. In fact Labouchere received somewhat conflicting recommendations from his two principal civil servants.

He closed the file with an ambiguous 'I concur' and signed a dispatch to the Governor saying that his refusal of Burt's appointment was confirmed but there was no reason to censure the Lieutenant-Governor for a step taken 'under a very natural misapprehension'.

This Henry Labouchere was, incidentally, the uncle of the Henry Labouchere who moved the notorious Labouchere Amendment to the 1885 Criminal Law Amendment Act, making illegal *all* male homosexual acts, not just buggery, whether committed in public or private.

The Colonial Office seems to have realised that a great injustice had been done to Burt. Before long Labouchere, the uncle, not the nephew, was writing to the Governor about a vacancy on the Bench in Jamaica and suggesting that this vacancy "could be made available for the promotion of Mr Burt".

But my great-great-grandfather was now caught in a *Catch-22* situation just over a hundred years before the publication of Joseph Heller's classic novel: In Jamaica you could not become a judge *unless* you had practised at the Bar of Jamaica or of the United Kingdom, the converse of the position in the Leeward

Islands, where you could not be made a judge *if* you had practised at the local bar.

With apparently no prospect of promotion in the West Indies, Burt wrote to the Duke of Newcastle, who by then had replaced Labouchere as Secretary of State for the Colonies, saying: "I am willing to serve the Crown in any of Her Majesty's possessions".

Nearly a year later, in April 1860, His Grace offered Burt the vacant positions of Civil Commissioner and Chairman of Quarter Sessions in Western Australia at a salary of £1000 a year. He accepted.

So, aged 49, Burt uprooted himself from St Kitts, leaving in June 1860 and travelling via Southampton to Australia, arriving at Fremantle on 29 January 1861. Before he left St Kitts, the House of Assembly unanimously voted him a gift of £500 as a mark of esteem; 750 ordinary people signed an address praising his service to the island, concluding "in you, the poor and distressed will lose a friend and a father"; and a public meeting presented him with a purse with which to buy, when he reached London, a candelabrum on which an inscription was to be made.

This candelabrum now belongs to Burt's great-great-grandson, Robert, who lives in Queensland. It is inscribed 'Presented in the year 1860 to the Honourable Archibald Paull Burt, Attorney-General of St Christopher's, by the inhabitants, in acknowledgment of the very great services rendered by him to the colony during a public life of twenty seven years'. *The Illustrated News of the World* for 22 September 1860 carried a large illustration of the candelabrum and a small news story, saying that it had been 'very elegantly executed by Messrs. Sarl, of Cornhill.'

Burt took five of his children with him to Australia: Septimus, Octavius, Alfred Earle, Francis Sinclair and Louisa Emily. His younger daughter, Mina, was not yet born. His eldest son, George Henry Burt (1837-1867), had joined the army, apparently in Jamaica, where four of his five children were born and where three of them died in infancy. He himself was only 30 when he died.

Burt's next two sons, Archibald Piguenit, then aged 21, and Frederick Augustus, then aged only 19, remained behind in St Kitts. Son number 6, Edmund Wigley Burt, was in the navy, and the fourth and fifth sons had already died.

Within six months of arriving in Western Australia, Archibald Paull Burt had become its first Chief Justice, a post to be held more than a hundred years later by his great-grandson, Sir Francis Burt, who eventually went one better and became Governor of Western Australia in 1990. They both had the Burt nose, mentioned earlier.

Archie had to wait 12 more years for his knighthood. His career has been fully and very readably described by Dr J M Bennett in *Sir Archibald Burt: First Chief Justice of Western Australia 1861-1879* (The Federation Press,

NSW, 2002, ISBN 1 86287 438 7). So I will leave him there, and move back a generation to his father.

The author's King grandparents and four of their five children, just before the first world war, perhaps in 1913: Iris, Milly, Howard (sitting on the floor), George Howard King, Rufus (Bryan) and Lilian Mary Burt. Harry was not born until 1921. Milly died when she was only five.

Louisa Emily Bryan
(1814-1870), who married
Archibald Paull Burt in 1836.
Her parents were Sarah Earle
Berkeley and Dr John Bryan

Alice Berridge (1846-1922),
who married Frederick
Augustus Burt in 1868. Her
parents were Thomas Probyn
Berridge and Maria Louisa
Kortright Aarestrup

Sir Archibald Paull Burt (1810-1879), who was Attorney-General of St Kitts before emigrating to Perth and becoming the first Chief Justice of Western Australia

Frederick Augustus Burt (1840-1912). The third of Sir Archibald's twelve children, he was only 20 when his father left St Kitts for Australia. He stayed behind to grow sugar cane

Alfred Earle Burt (1852-1935), Sir Archibald's ninth son, who worked in his brother Septimus' law office and then as clerk to his father, the Chief Justice of Western Australia. He was eventually appointed Registrar of Titles in the Land Titles Department in Perth

Captain Edmund Wigley Burt RN (1846-1926), the sixth son of Archibald Paull Burt and Louisa Emily Bryan. He was born in St Kitts and died on the Isle of Wight, where he was Captain of the Coast Guard at Ventnor

Five Birches, sisters and cousins, in 1962. Standing: Grace Garland (Pots) Birch (1895-1977) and Ernestine Frances (Nesta) Birch (1881-1970). Seated: Rosalie Muriel Birch (1898-1978), Marion Eleanor Birch (1884-1968) and Constance Ellen Birch (1897-1980). Grace and Con were the daughters of Ernest Albert Birch; the other three were the daughters of Edward Alfred Birch

Harry: Henry Maitland King (1921-1975) during the second world war, perhaps about 1943. He was profoundly affected by the war and after his demobilisation had three nervous breakdowns. He was St Kitts' very first community welfare officer and died at the age of 53.

Rufus: Bryan Earle King (1906-1987) as a young Fellow of Pembroke College, Cambridge, probably in the late 1930s. He was said to have 'the third finest legal brain in Europe' and was elected a Fellow of his college when he was only 21. He was the British Council's first representative in Barbados and later helped to set up the West Indian Students' Centre in London

George Peyton Gregory (1836-1911), the author's cabinet-maker great-grandfather. In his Kenilworth workshop, he employed several men in the manufacture of sound, solid, well-designed furniture. Later he was a partner in an auctioneer and estate agent business in Southsea, but the venture failed

Aunty Nan: Rosena Annie Gregory (1872-1968). She kept a shop in Portishead, selling stationery, sweets, toys and tobacco. She taught herself to read when she was three and was still doing the crossword puzzle in the *Western Daily Press* at the time of this photograph when she was 91. She died as mentally alert as ever, when she was 95

Agnes Adelaide Frederica Lissolo Birch
(1893-1923), known as Rica, at her piano.
She married Arthur Edward Emms in 1920.
Miriam was their daughter. Rica was a
brilliant musician; she played with the
Bournemouth Symphony under Dan Godfrey
and had an audition with Sir Henry Wood,
who engaged her to play at a Promenade
Concert. She died when she was 30

Ernestine Margery Birch (1902-1979) at
her loom in Paradise Cottage, near Truro.
She was the author's favourite aunt. She
worked as a handweaver before the war
and then served for six years in the
Women's Auxilliary Air Force. After the
war she was a flower farmer in the Isles
of Scilly. When she was 50, she married
Stephen Lewis Hicks. He was then 69,
and he survived her

The author's Birch grandparents, their children and their nephew, taken in about 1907, perhaps at 10 Freemantle Square, Bristol. Back row: Bernard, Grace, Reggie Morphew and Con. Front row: Norman, Harriette Elizabeth Gregory (Birch), Margery and Ernest Albert Birch. Reggie had been added to the family, without any consultation with his aunt, because his father drank

The author's parents, probably in Teddington in 1930, when they were on leave in England from the West Indies: Iris Berkeley King (1905-1988) and Norman Peyton Birch (1890-1950)

Chapter 9

George Henry Burt and his forbears

Very rich sugar planters
with lots of slaves

Sir Archibald Burt was the public servant *par excellence*; his father was an extremely wealthy sugar planter.

George Henry Burt (the first of several George Henry Burts) was born on 17 May 1787 and died on 10 October 1851.

I have visited his grave in St Paul's churchyard, St Kitts. There is a marble cross to his memory and to that of his soldier grandson, another George Henry Burt (1837-1867). Another of his grandsons, my great-grandfather Frederick Augustus Burt (1840-1912), and Frederick's daughter Helena Maud Burt are buried nearby. She was only six when she died.

The second George Henry Burt (1809-1846), first-born of the first GHB, is also buried at St Paul's. The fourth GHB, elder son of the third, died and was buried in Jamaica.

The first George Henry Burt owned and lived in style at Brotherson's Estate. In 1831 he owned 129 slaves. In 1834 he still had 129 slaves, an increase of 14 by birth and a decrease of 14 -- "three seized and condemned to [sic] His Majesty by [sic] death, 11 died (1 condemned to death, pardoned but since dead)".

When he entertained the officers from Brimstone Hill at Brotherson's, a large tablecloth of linen damask with the Burt coat of arms (*Argent, on a chevron gules between three bugle-horns stringed sable, as many crosses crosslet of the first*) woven in it would be spread on the wide lawn, in the middle of which stood an enormous evergreen tree.

When he returned from one of his visits to England, he brought with him twelve handsome mahogany chests with brass edges, locks and name plates -- all filled with linen.

There is no doubt that my great-great-great-grandfather was seriously rich. He was also Road Surveyor of St Kitts and Speaker of the House of Assembly. And he had three very beautiful daughters, so beautiful that they were known as the Three Graces, after the daughters of Zeus and Eurynome, who sang and danced for the gods and who were captured in marble by the neo-classical sculptor, Antonio Canova.

Not surprisingly, they all married: Eliza Pitcher married Francis Spencer Wigley the Elder, Sarah Lynch married John Earle Tudor, and Anna Louisa married Steuart Spencer Davis.

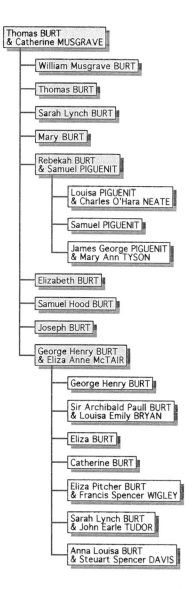

Thomas BURT
& Catherine MUSGRAVE

- William Musgrave BURT
- Thomas BURT
- Sarah Lynch BURT
- Mary BURT
- Rebekah BURT
  & Samuel PIGUENIT
  - Louisa PIGUENIT
    & Charles O'Hara NEATE
  - Samuel PIGUENIT
  - James George PIGUENIT
    & Mary Ann TYSON
- Elizabeth BURT
- Samuel Hood BURT
- Joseph BURT
- George Henry BURT
  & Eliza Anne McTAIR
  - George Henry BURT
  - Sir Archibald Paull BURT
    & Louisa Emily BRYAN
  - Eliza BURT
  - Catherine BURT
  - Eliza Pitcher BURT
    & Francis Spencer WIGLEY
  - Sarah Lynch BURT
    & John Earle TUDOR
  - Anna Louisa BURT
    & Steuart Spencer DAVIS

Thomas Burt and his forbears

The first George Henry Burt's father was Thomas Burt, who was born in 1733.
In February 1767 he married Catherine Musgrave. George Henry, born 20
years later, was their ninth child.

We are now in the middle of the 18th century, and the information about my family that I have managed to gather is getting thinner. I know a lot of names and dates but, in many cases, not much more. Several of the earlier Burts held important offices in the colonial system, but I know nothing about Thomas except his dates and the fact that he was a prominent member of the community. I don't know how he lived or how he supported his wife and nine children.

But I discovered that his widow Catherine (born: 28 October 1749) registered as his executrix in 1817 five slaves:

William	male	black	50	Creole of Nevis	house servant
Nelly	female	black	22	Creole of St Kitts	house servant
Phillis	female	black	38	Afrn Mandingo	cook
Jim	male	black	5	Creole of St Kitts	none
Ben	male	black	3	Creole of St Kitts	none

And I can tell you that Thomas was the second son of Charles Pym Burt and his wife Rebekah Woolley, and Charles was a member of the Nevis Council in 1753 and must therefore have been a man of some wealth.

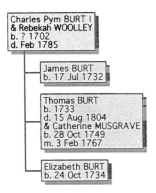

I don't even know when Charles Pym Burt was born or when he died but his three children were born between July 1732 and October 1734. His father died in 1707 and had seven children after Charles so I would guess that he was born towards the end of the 17th century and died before the end of the 18th. It seems that he lived in Nevis, as his son James and his daughter Elizabeth were both baptised at St John's, Fig Tree, where Nelson's marriage certificate is displayed and where my mother is said to have been baptised.

The President of Nevis
Charles Pym Burt was the third son of Colonel William Burt and Elizabeth Pym. William was born about 1640. He was a member of the Council of Nevis in 1692 and 1693, and became President in 1699. This was quite an important

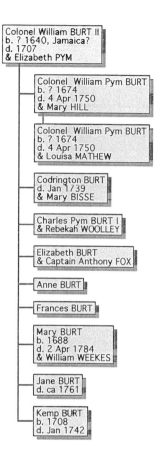

Colonel William BURT II
b. ? 1640, Jamaica?
d. 1707
& Elizabeth PYM

Colonel William Pym BURT
b. ? 1674
d. 4 Apr 1750
& Mary HILL

Colonel William Pym BURT
b. ? 1674
d. 4 Apr 1750
& Louisa MATHEW

Codrington BURT
d. Jan 1739
& Mary BISSE

Charles Pym BURT I
& Rebekah WOOLLEY

Elizabeth BURT
& Captain Anthony FOX

Anne BURT

Frances BURT

Mary BURT
b. 1688
d. 2 Apr 1784
& William WEEKES

Jane BURT
d. ca 1761

Kemp BURT
b. 1708
d. Jan 1742

post. The original headquarters of the Leeward Islands, under Sir Thomas Warner, had been St Kitts, but Nevis succeeded to this honour after the destruction of the English colony in St Kitts by the French in 1666. For many years Nevis was the most important and prosperous island in the group.

And if both the Governor of the Leewards and the Lieutenant-Governor of Nevis were away, the President of Nevis took over the administration of the Leeward Islands.

Colonel William Burt owned the Tower Hill Estate of 240 acres in the parish of St Thomas in Nevis, and his will, made in October 1707, shows that he had plenty of sugar to dispose of.

To my daus. Eliz. wife of Anthony Fox, Anne Burt, Frances B., Mary B. and Jane B. 40,000 lbs. of sugar each. Wife with child, if a boy 50,000, if a girl 40,000 lbs. To my sons Codrington B. and Cha. Pym B. 50,000 lbs each. My wife Eliz. one-third of my estate in lieu of dower, plate during life, and a negro woman. All residue to my s. Wm. B. and sole Ex'or.

William Burt's wife Elizabeth came from another influential and wealthy West Indian family. She was the youngest daughter of Colonel Charles Pym, who was born in 1650, the eldest son of Thomas Pym of Bristol. The family was rich enough to send Charles to Oxford University when he was 15, and by the 1670s he owned a plantation on Nevis.

According to my handwritten Burt family tree, Colonel William Burt married twice and his second wife is given as 'Jane Pym, daughter of Colonel Charles Pym of Nevis', with no name for his first wife. And it shows his eldest son, also William Burt, married to Elizabeth Pym. This is in line with the Pym family tree in volume III of *Caribbeana*, which shows 'Jane Pym, mar Col Wm Burt of Nevis (as his 2nd wife)' and her younger sister 'Eliz Pym, mar Wm Burt of Nevis, son of Col Wm Burt'.

This is all very confusing. At first glance, one might assume that Elizabeth had married her sister's son. But the Colonel William Burt who seems to have married Jane Pym was the son of an earlier Colonel William Burt. So the 'Wm Burt of Nevis' whom Eliz married could have been the same Colonel William Burt who married sister Jane, and my old family tree may contain a mistaken and superfluous generation. Are you still with me?

However, the second Colonel William Burt's will, made shortly before his death in 1707, mentions his wife Elizabeth, so Jane could hardly have been his second wife. It is a mystery that may never be solved.

Susan Morris of Debrett Ancestry Research Ltd concludes that "possibly Jane was his first wife, but it is more likely that the names have become confused".

Be that as it may, Elizabeth Pym's brother, another Charles Pym, left a will dated 13 December 1739, which mentions some of his Burt relations: and gives something of the flavour of the life of rich West Indian planters in the 18th century:

To old Will his freedom and 2 barrels of beef yearly. My mulatto girl Bussy her freedom and £300 c at 21, and £20 c till then. Mrs Jane Burt £500 c if living in my house at my death. Cha Pym Weatherill, son of Jas W Esq .... at 21. My godson Cha Pym Burt, son of Wm Pym B Esq, of St Chrs, £500 at 21. My goddau Fra Pym Douglas, dau of John D Esq, of St Chrs, £500 at 21 or mar. My niece Mrs Eliz Fox, wid, of Montserrat, £300 c. Hospital for Found Chn in Gt B, now about to be founded, £100. Poor of Old Road £100 c. My dau Priscilla Pym all residue and sole h and Ex'trix, but to be in T till 21 or mar, and if she die under 21 and sp to my good friend Col Vallentine Morris £1000 st, and Wm Pym Burt, James Browne, and Jno Spooner Snr Esqres and Capt Syer Alklicocke £500 each, and to Mrs Deborah Smith £100, and all res to my neph Wm Pym Burt and to Col Val Morris eq. My good friends John Willet Sr, Jeremiah Browne, and Wm Pym Burt of St Chr Esqres, and Sam Hawkes of Montserrat, Mercht, Ex'ors in T and £100 each. Wit by John Frank, Wm Panton, Tho Pellet. (132, Spurway)

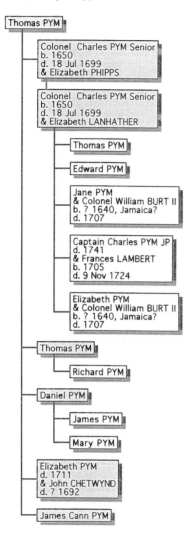

Thomas PYM

Colonel Charles PYM Senior
b. 1650
d. 18 Jul 1699
& Elizabeth PHIPPS

Colonel Charles PYM Senior
b. 1650
d. 18 Jul 1699
& Elizabeth LANHATHER

Thomas PYM

Edward PYM

Jane PYM
& Colonel William BURT II
b. ? 1640, Jamaica?
d. 1707

Captain Charles PYM JP
d. 1741
& Frances LAMBERT
b. 1705
d. 9 Nov 1724

Elizabeth PYM
& Colonel William BURT II
b. ? 1640, Jamaica?
d. 1707

Thomas PYM

Richard PYM

Daniel PYM

James PYM

Mary PYM

Elizabeth PYM
d. 1711
& John CHETWYND
d. ? 1692

James Cann PYM

The will was proved on 16 April 1741 by Charles Pym's daughter, the Rt Hon Priscilla, Lady Romney. Priscilla was the granddaughter of Major-General Lambert, the Lieutenant Governor of St Kitts. Priscilla's father-in-law, the fifth baronet and the first Lord Romney, had been Governor of Dover Castle and MP for Maidstone. And Priscilla's son Charles was successively MP for Maidstone and Kent and eventually Lord Lieutenant of Kent. He was the third Baron Romney and in 1801 was created Viscount Marsham and Earl of Romney.

Colonel Charles Pym's father is shown in *Caribbeana* as 'Tho. Pym of Bristol, "pleb."'. Less than 100 years and only two generations of sugar-cane planters later, the plebeian Thomas' great-granddaughter had married into the aristocracy.

But we must leave the Pyms and return to the Burts.

The first Burt

According to *Caribbeana*, "The family of Burt occupied from early days a very prominent position in the Leeward Islands". The first Burt that I know about was the father of the Colonel William Burt who married Elizabeth and possibly also Jane Pym. Confusingly, as already mentioned, he was also a William and also a Colonel. But while the son was President of Nevis at the time of his death in 1707, the father was Deputy Governor when he died in 1686.

According to V L Oliver's *The History of Antigua* (vol I, 1894, page 90), Burt signed a petition of the Leeward Island planters in 1670. The 1678 census of Nevis shows the then Captain William Burt having

7 white men, 1 do woman, 6 do children, 16 negro men, 17 women and 15 children.

That year he was promoted Major and became Deputy Governor of the Leeward Islands seven years later in 1685. At about that time, before he died in 1686, he was given 100,000 lb of sugar by the Assembly. At any rate Sir Nathaniel Johnson, the new Governor of the Leeward Islands,

"wrote in 1687 that in reference to the present of 100,000 lbs the Assembly had voted to Col Wm Burt he could ascertain but little, as Col Burt died before his arrival, and his Ex'ors and friends pretended ignorance, but Burt had done His Majesty good service." (17, Colonial Entry Book)

I have no doubt that my ancestor did good service to the king in addition to looking after his own interests, but why the huge gift of sugar and why should his executors and friends have pretended ignorance of it?

It seems that Burt may have been a planter in Jamaica before moving to Nevis. A William Burt owned 110 acres in St Andrew's parish in Jamaica in 1670, and two of his daughters were baptised at St Andrew's, Elizabeth in 1669 and Dorcas in 1672. But before then?

A list of 'passengers embarking from the Port of London on the *Bonaventure* bound to Barbados and St Christophers Islands' on 6 January 1635 contains a

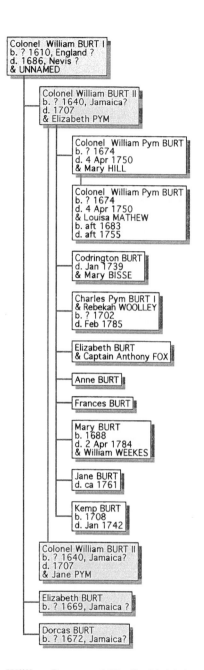

Colonel William BURT I
b. ? 1610, England ?
d. 1686, Nevis ?
& UNNAMED

Colonel William BURT II
b. ? 1640, Jamaica?
d. 1707
& Elizabeth PYM

Colonel William Pym BURT
b. ? 1674
d. 4 Apr 1750
& Mary HILL

Colonel William Pym BURT
b. ? 1674
d. 4 Apr 1750
& Louisa MATHEW
b. aft 1683
d. aft 1755

Codrington BURT
d. Jan 1739
& Mary BISSE

Charles Pym BURT I
& Rebekah WOOLLEY
b. ? 1702
d. Feb 1785

Elizabeth BURT
& Captain Anthony FOX

Anne BURT

Frances BURT

Mary BURT
b. 1688
d. 2 Apr 1784
& William WEEKES

Jane BURT
d. ca 1761

Kemp BURT
b. 1708
d. Jan 1742

Colonel William BURT II
b. ? 1640, Jamaica?
d. 1707
& Jane PYM

Elizabeth BURT
b. ? 1669, Jamaica ?

Dorcas BURT
b. ? 1672, Jamaica?

William Burt, aged 22. Could this have been my 7 x great-grandfather?

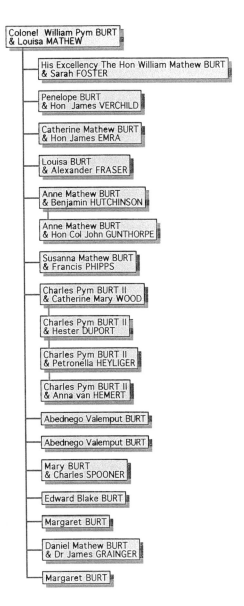

Colonel William Pym BURT
& Louisa MATHEW

His Excellency The Hon William Mathew BURT
& Sarah FOSTER

Penelope BURT
& Hon James VERCHILD

Catherine Mathew BURT
& Hon James EMRA

Louisa BURT
& Alexander FRASER

Anne Mathew BURT
& Benjamin HUTCHINSON

Anne Mathew BURT
& Hon Col John GUNTHORPE

Susanna Mathew BURT
& Francis PHIPPS

Charles Pym BURT II
& Catherine Mary WOOD

Charles Pym BURT II
& Hester DUPORT

Charles Pym BURT II
& Petronella HEYLIGER

Charles Pym BURT II
& Anna van HEMERT

Abednego Valemput BURT

Abednego Valemput BURT

Mary BURT
& Charles SPOONER

Edward Blake BURT

Margaret BURT

Daniel Mathew BURT
& Dr James GRAINGER

Margaret BURT

'A Particular List of persons paid their first month's pay for their respective Qualities under the Command of General Venables in the West Indies, December 1654' includes a William Burt as a drummer in Haines Companye (PRO Colonial Papers, vol 32, no 16). Did this drummer rise to the rank of colonel and become Deputy Governor of Nevis? I would dearly love to know, but I don't. That is as far back into history as I can trace nine of my direct ancestors on my mother's side. The first William Burt was born about 1610, probably in England but I know not where.

A Chief Justice and four Governors
There are, however, several other Burts on the family tree, collateral not direct ancestors, who are worthy of inclusion in the family story. I will now turn around and start to move forward in time from the end of the 17th century.

Charles Pym Burt's eldest brother, Colonel William Pym Burt, was born around 1674, probably in Nevis. He moved to St Kitts in 1725, became Chief Justice there and died in 1750 or 1751. He married twice. His second wife was Louisa Mathew, youngest daughter of Sir William Mathew, Captain General of the Leeward Islands. Her grandfather was the Hon Abednego Mathew, the Governor of the Leeward Islands.

William Pym Burt had two, possibly three daughters by his first wife and a further 14 children by his second wife, Louisa. The eldest of these was William Mathew Burt who moved to England from St Kitts, acquired a country estate at Maiden Earley in Berkshire, and became MP for Great Marlow. His maiden speech on 25 November 1762 is described in *The History of Parliament Trust (1754-1790)* as 'dull as far as could be heard' and it appears that his subsequent speeches were no better.

In 1768 he contested Great Marlow again but was badly defeated. In 1776, he was appointed Captain General and Commander in Chief of His Majesty's Leeward Islands and remained Governor until his death in Antigua in 1781. His will mentions 'my negroes at St Christophers to be treated as real estate'.

My maternal grandfather, George King, wrote an article about him in *The St Kitts-Nevis Daily Bulletin* of 24 December 1936, which starts: "In the long list of our rulers we have had many that are scarce worth remembering and a few that may be called men of character. Among the latter may be named William Matthew Burt ...."

The Mathew is sometimes spelt with one t, sometimes with two. And the top job in the colonies at that time was sometimes called Governor, sometimes Captain General. It is interesting that William Mathew Burt and his mother's father and grandfather all held the top job in the Leeward Islands.

Not only that. WMB's sister Penelope married the Hon James Verchild, who was Governor of the Leeward Islands from 1766 to 1769. They had 13 children. Huge families, immense wealth, plenty of slaves and most of the top jobs, that seems to have been the picture.

[*The chart on the previous page shows two children's names twice. This is not a mistake. The first Abednego died aged one, and the first Margaret died aged two, and their parents used the same names a second time.*]

Chapter 10

The poet, the Prince of Wales and the Field-Marshal

*Dr Johnson's ridicule, an illegal marriage,
the Chief of Staff of the Prussian Army,
some seafaring Burts and the Piguenit family*

Two more of the 14 children of Col William Pym Burt and Louisa Mathew should be included in the story. Another of WMB's sisters with the misleadingly masculine name of Daniel Mathew Burt married the poet James Grainger who wrote a long poem on the cultivation of the sugar cane, which was ridiculed by Dr Johnson: 'One might as well write "The Parsley-Bed, a Poem" or "The Cabbage-Garden, a Poem"'.

James Boswell in *The Life of Samuel Johnson* describes how Grainger had been persuaded by a West-India gentleman, a Mr Bourryau, to accompany him to the West Indies. 'He accordingly embarked with the gentleman; but upon the voyage fell in love with a young woman, Miss Burt, who happened to be one of the passengers, and married the wench'.

WMB's brother Charles Pym Burt (not to be confused with the Charles Pym Burt who married Rebekah Woolley -- and there are two more Charles Pym Burts not yet mentioned) had four wives.

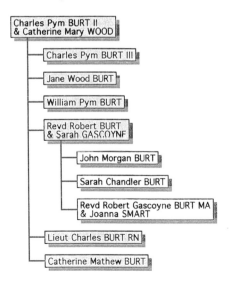

Charles Pym BURT II
& Catherine Mary WOOD
— Charles Pym BURT III
— Jane Wood BURT
— William Pym BURT
— Revd Robert BURT
& Sarah GASCOYNE
— John Morgan BURT
— Sarah Chandler BURT
— Revd Robert Gascoyne BURT MA
& Joanna SMART
— Lieut Charles BURT RN
— Catherine Mathew BURT

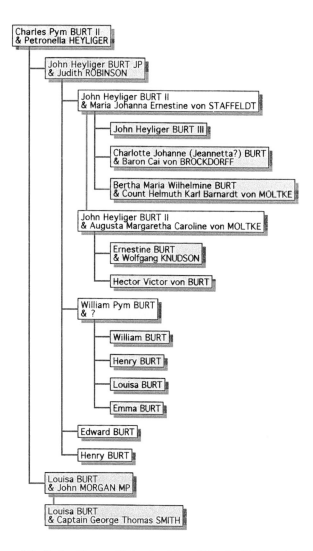

Charles Pym BURT II
& Petronella HEYLIGER

John Heyliger BURT JP
& Judith ROBINSON

John Heyliger BURT II
& Maria Johanna Ernestine von STAFFELDT

John Heyliger BURT III

Charlotte Johanne (Jeannetta?) BURT
& Baron Cai von BROCKDORFF

Bertha Maria Wilhelmine BURT
& Count Helmuth Karl Barnardt von MOLTKE

John Heyliger BURT II
& Augusta Margaretha Caroline von MOLTKE

Ernestine BURT
& Wolfgang KNUDSON

Hector Victor von BURT

William Pym BURT
& ?

William BURT

Henry BURT

Louisa BURT

Emma BURT

Edward BURT

Henry BURT

Louisa BURT
& John MORGAN MP

Louisa BURT
& Captain George Thomas SMITH

His first wife was Catherine Mary Wood of Middleham Castle, Yorkshire, and one of their six children was to become a footnote in the history books as the clergyman who secretly and illegally married the Prince of Wales to Mrs Maria Fitzherbert in the latter's drawing room in 1785.

This was the Rev Rober Burt, Vicar of Twickenham, who has been most unfairly treated by historians, it being suggested that he was a down-at-heel nonentity bailed out of the Fleet Prison and his debts paid so that he could perform the marriage service.

This story has been repeated in many books about Mrs Fitzherbert and King George IV and even in the Alan Bennett film *The Madness of King George*, but the records of the Fleet Prison contain no trace of his name.

And there is no reason to think he would have been penniless. He had a very wealthy father and, just 18 months before the wedding, he had been appointed one of the four Chaplains in Ordinary to the Prince of Wales.

When I raised the matter with Alan Bennett, he sent me an apologetic post-card saying: "I'm afraid I just made it all up! We needed a scene at the last moment so I did no research whatsoever. Sorry!".

Charles Pym Burt's second wife, Hester Duport, died without producing any more little Burts, but his third wife, Petronella Heyliger, gave him two. The elder, John Heyliger Burt, became High Sherrif of Staffordshire in 1805, and JHB's granddaughter, Bertha Marie Wilhelmine Burt married Helmuth Karl Bernhardt Graf von Moltke the day he became a Major in the Prussian army. Helmuth was eventually to become a Field-Marshal and was Chief of the General Staff of the Prussian army at the time of the Austro-Prussian and Franco-Prussian wars.

The Prussian Field-Marshal and his West Indian wife are buried in the chapel at the von Moltke schloss at Creisau, near Schweidnitz in Silesia. I have photographs of their graves.

The seafaring Burts
Charles Pym Burt's fourth wife, Anna van Hemert, produced five more children, making his total 13. One of these, Edward, entered the Navy in 1795

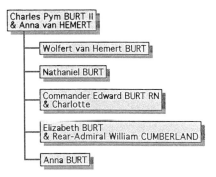

at the age of 17 and eventually rose to the rank of Commander. I have a slim, pale green volume with gilt-edged pages he published in 1844 entitled *The Hurricane: A Poem*. It is described on the title-page as

Descriptive of the unparalleled perseverance and constancy of the Seamen on board H M Ship *Theseus*, 74 guns, commanded by Captain (now Rear-Admiral) E Hawker, the flag-ship of the late Rear-Admiral Dacres, during three days' and nights' hurricane, which, in company with the *Hercule*, she encountered North-East of Monte Christi, in the Island of St Domingo.

Edward's introduction modestly begins: 'In the following pages a feeble effort is made to describe, in rhyme-verse, the hurricane ...'. It ends: 'The writer hopes the originality of his style -- his comparisons of land with sea life -- and his incidental allusions to occurrences at and about St Domingo, may be charitably received. His veneration for literature would deter him from willingly offending. E. B., Commander, R.N.'

Although Edward Burt's full name is nowhere given in the book, he is undoubtedly the author. In the 'Reminiscences' that follow the poem, he mentions that Captain Cumberland, commander of the frigate *Pique*, was his brother-in-law and a little later he tells of a conversation with Henry Christophe, the former slave from St Kitts who became King of Haiti.

It was upon this occasion that he told me he was born at St Christopher's, whence he was named. For the first time during my intercourse with him, he asked if I was related to his late Excellency the Governor-General of our West-Indian dependencies; I acquainted him he was my uncle; when he stopped, and, taking my hand, told me he was venerated, and justly so, as a good man, whilst it afforded infinite gratification to him to have met any relative to whom he could testify his esteem.

The Governor-General was, of course, Edward's uncle, William Mathew Burt, and Captain (later Rear-Admiral) William Cumberland married Edward's sister Elizabeth.

Edward had nine daughters, one of whom, Fanny, married Admiral Sir Henry Trollope.

Another seafaring Burt was my great-grandfather's younger brother, Captain Edmund Wigley Burt RN (1846-1926), who died on the Isle of Wight, where

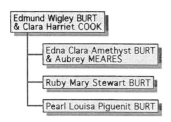

his widow, Aunt Clara, continued to live for 16 years after his death. I visited her and two of her daughters during our big family holiday on the island in the summer of 1938. The three daughters were named after battleships, Amethyst, Ruby and Pearl, but had other names as well. Edna Clara Amethyst married

Aubrey Meares, and left home. Their son John was another sailor and rose to be Commander RN before being invalided out of the Navy. When the Fleet visited St Kitts in March 1938, he invited me to tea with him on his battleship and sent the Admiral's launch to fetch me from the Basseterre pier.

The other two sisters, whom I knew as Ruby and Piggy, never married and were still living at home with Aunt Clara in 1938. Piggy was short for Piguenit, her full name being Pearl Louisa Piguenit.

The Piguenit family

George Henry Burt's sister Rebekah had married a Samuel Piguenit in St Kitts in 1795. And their son, James George Piguenit, was the lawyer who defended (unsuccessfully) a gang of pirates who were hanged in Basseterre in 1828.

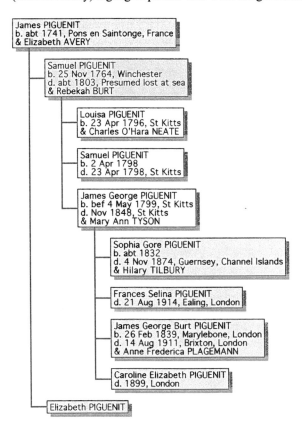

The Piguenits, a French Protestant family from Pons, an ancient town lying between La Rochelle and Bordeaux, sought refuge in England after the revocation of the Edict of Nantes in 1685 opened the door to renewed persecution of the Protestants. They had settled in Bristol by 1702.

Rebekah's husband Samuel was the eldest son of James Piguenit, who had been born in Pons around 1741. It is possible that his immediate family stayed on in France, pretending to follow the Catholic faith, escaping eventually to relatives in Bristol in the mid 1700s when circumstances again worsened in France for secret Protestants. Or James' father could have been one of the Bristol Piguenits, who went back to France at some point when persecution eased to look after some property and then had to get out again after James was born.

Anyhow, James was apprenticed as an upholsterer, probably in Bristol, and by the age of 22 was living in Southampton, where in February 1764 he married Elizabeth Avery. Almost exactly nine months later, in November, Samuel was born. Samuel seems to have been of a restless disposition and in 1787 signed on as the servant of the second mate on the maiden voyage of one of the East India Company's ships bound for China.

He returned to England the following year and joined the Royal Navy, appearing in St Kitts in 1795 where he was married to Rebekah Burt, one of the nine children of Thomas and Catherine Burt, one of the leading families of the island. There were three children of this marriage, the youngest of whom, James George Piguenit, was born in 1798. Soon after his birth, Samuel disappeared from the scene. Family tradition says that he was lost at sea in an encounter with the French.

At about this time, one of Samuel's sisters, Anne, apparently on a visit to the island, died and was buried in St George's churchyard. She was only 20.

James George Piguenit studied law and, as a young barrister in St Kitts, was assigned the unenviable task of defending the pirate captain de Buysan, who was convicted with most of his crew of piracy on the high seas and hanged in Basseterre at Pond's Pasture in September 1828.

JGP's son, James George Burt Piguenit, was a Puisne Judge in St Kitts later in the century. And JGBP's daughter Haidee Irene Piguenit was the mother of Denis Lacy-Hulbert, known as Ben, whom I have met several times and who is living, aged 92, in Devizes as I write this.

Another Piguenit, Frederick, was transported to Tasmania in 1830 after being sentenced at the Warwick Assizes to 14 years in jail for 'a misdemeanour' involving 'a most extensive robbery of government stores from his Majesty's Dock-yard at Chatham'. His son, William Charles Piguenit (1836-1914), was, I believe, a distinguished Australian artist.

Two suicides

As far as I know, only two members of my family have taken their own lives. My grandmother's older brother, Probyn Berridge Burt, killed himself, aged

25, in 1878. As already mentioned, it seems that he was in love with a Miss MacArthur and that she did not fully reciprocate his feelings. Anyhow, the Fleet was in and, when Probyn saw Miss MacArthur's carriage drive past his door bearing her to a ball on one of the warships, he shot himself.

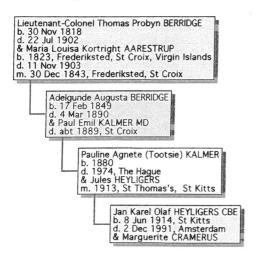

Lieutenant-Colonel Thomas Probyn BERRIDGE
b. 30 Nov 1818
d. 22 Jul 1902
& Maria Louisa Kortright AARESTRUP
b. 1823, Frederiksted, St Croix, Virgin Islands
d. 11 Nov 1903
m. 30 Dec 1843, Frederiksted, St Croix

Adelgunde Augusta BERRIDGE
b. 17 Feb 1849
d. 4 Mar 1890
& Paul Emil KALMER MD
d. abt 1889, St Croix

Pauline Agnete (Tootsie) KALMER
b. 1880
d. 1974, The Hague
& Jules HEYLIGERS
m. 1913, St Thomas's, St Kitts

Jan Karel Olaf HEYLIGERS CBE
b. 8 Jun 1914, St Kitts
d. 2 Dec 1991, Amsterdam
& Marguerite CRAMERUS

And in 1991 my third cousin, once removed, Jan Karel Olaf Heyligers, committed suicide in the Netherlands. Olaf was born in St Kitts and became Head of the Public Services Department in Amsterdam. In 1975 he was made a honorary Commander of the British Empire, and the insignia were presented to him by Queen Elizabeth the Queen Mother at a ceremony at the British Embassy in the Hague.

Olaf had served as chairman of the Appeal Committee for the restoration of the English Reform Church in Amsterdam and was also Vice-President of the Netherlands-England Society. The CBE was in recognition of this work. I made contact with Olaf in 1987, when I wrote to tell him of Rufus' death, and helped him with some advice when he visited St Kitts for the last time in November that year.

The formal announcement of his decease said: "With deep regret we have to inform you of the sudden death, after several months' illness bravely borne, of our very dear husband, father, father-in-law and grandfather ...". His widow wrote to me: "Olaf made himself an end to a hopeless illness of several months. Your Xmas card came too late. Thank you nevertheless. Marguerite".

Chapter 11

The Berridges and the Danish connection

*The Treasurer of St Kitts, the Chamberlain to the King of Denmark
and the mysteries of Christian Aarestrup's mother
and the Master of Pembroke College*

Olaf's great-grandfather and my great-great-grandfather was Thomas Probyn
Berridge, the father of Alice Berridge, mentioned earlier. Standing on the
bookcase in my study is a silver-gilt beaker inscribed 'Berridge 1843-1893' to
mark the 50th wedding anniversary of Thomas Probyn and Maria Louisa Kortright Aarestrup. I get a thrill from owning and holding a 110-year-old artefact
that used to belong to my great-great-grandparents.

I also have 38 of their silver spoons and forks with the reeded fiddle pattern
and the Berridge crest of a Cornish chough. They bear the H and I date letters,
indicating 1843 and 1844 respectively. We use them regularly. And on my
mantelpiece are the box spurs worn by my great-great-grandfather as Colonel
of the St Kitts militia.

Thomas Probyn Berridge was born in 1818, and his mother died three weeks
after his birth, leaving him in the care of his sister Eliza. He was sent to school
in Salisbury 'under Dr Radcliffe' in 1831. Thomas played the flute and sang in
the Salisbury Cathedral choir. I therefore assumed that he had been at the
Salisbury Cathedral School, but there is no record of him or of Dr Radcliffe
having been there. However, there was a Revd George Radcliffe who ran a
gentlemen's boarding school in Castle Street, not far from the cathedral, and
that is probably where he was educated.

His schoolboy notebooks reveal many of the characteristics of his later life.
He carefully noted down all the presents he received: "Ten shillings from my
Father, ten shillings from Mitchell Chapman, £1 from Dr Swanston". And he
recorded what he spent and all sums lent to other boys.

He returned to St Kitts in 1837, 'tall, handsome, broad-shouldered, full of
joie de vivre, kindly, generous, winning', although it is not clear from my
family papers who described him thus. His principal loves were music and
horses.

In 1838 he wrote to his elder brother James, who was completing his education at Trinity Hall, Cambridge, while his business partner, Mr Wade, was
becoming restive.

November 9th 1838. I have lately been to Heldens, which is looking miserably bad.
The present manager appears to me a lazy fellow. I am sure when you come you

92

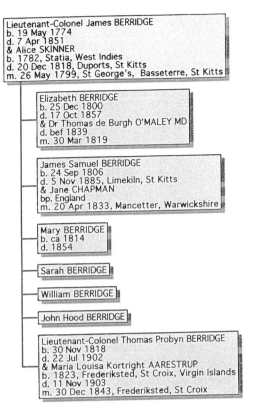

Lieutenant-Colonel James BERRIDGE
b. 19 May 1774
d. 7 Apr 1851
& Alice SKINNER
b. 1782, Statia, West Indies
d. 20 Dec 1818, Duports, St Kitts
m. 26 May 1799, St George's, Basseterre, St Kitts

Elizabeth BERRIDGE
b. 25 Dec 1800
d. 17 Oct 1857
& Dr Thomas de Burgh O'MALEY MD
d. bef 1839
m. 30 Mar 1819

James Samuel BERRIDGE
b. 24 Sep 1806
d. 5 Nov 1885, Limekiln, St Kitts
& Jane CHAPMAN
bp. England
m. 20 Apr 1833, Mancetter, Warwickshire

Mary BERRIDGE
b. ca 1814
d. 1854

Sarah BERRIDGE

William BERRIDGE

John Hood BERRIDGE

Lieutenant-Colonel Thomas Probyn BERRIDGE
b. 30 Nov 1818
d. 22 Jul 1902
& Maria Louisa Kortright AARESTRUP
b. 1823, Frederiksted, St Croix, Virgin Islands
d. 11 Nov 1903
m. 30 Dec 1843, Frederiksted, St Croix

will find it requesite to reside a month or two on the estate, because by your presence the negroes will reform and become more moral and industrious. I have not been to Spooners yet, but understand that you have a fine gang of labourers....Tell Jane I have got such a pretty little thorough-bred English horse for her to ride when she comes out. At present it is very spirited, but I think by the time you come out it will be quieter. I changed another horse with Wade for a little chestnut, which I have raced about five times this year and won all the Cups. Nothing has beaten him as yet, but he is an ugly dog and will not keep fat upon 10 pints of oats a day although he is a very good horse to ride, so I have bought this blood which is a valuable horse. I gave £50 stg for him. I am only afraid that when you come out you will be too apt to fall in love with him....I wish you would either bring or send the following pieces of Music for me, viz: Handel's Messiah, Beethoven's Hallelujah Chorus [*sic*], Handel's Overtures .... Please send them as I am anxious for them in order that we may know some of them before Jane comes. Mary *squalls* away every Sunday in Church. The Vestry have sent the Organ to England for repairs....I am writing to Mr Scargill. One of my Bootmakers, a Mr Dollman, has been very insolent to him, and I shall accordingly dismiss him.

This letter was written when Probyn was three weeks short of his 20th birthday. Like his schoolboy notebooks, it gives a foretaste of the man he was to become. In *Strings and Pipe*, the story of the building of the organ in St George's Church, Basseterre, in 1872, the late George Walker describes him thus:

> The chief protagonist for the erection of a new organ was a leading vestryman, Thomas Probyn Berridge. Berridge was at the time one of the Colony's most distinguished citizens. A prominent business man with interests in sugar and other merchandise and the proprietor of a rum distillery, he was also Colonel of the local Militia, a leader in local society and well known as a music lover.
>
> The Berridge family lived in considerable state at Dewars, an estate house a little west of Basseterre close by the estate house of his elder brother James Berridge who had recently become the President of the island's Legislative Assembly.
>
> Probyn Berridge and his large family also used from time to time the fine town house of the Berridge family which still stands in Pall Mall Square. The decision to commission an organ was taken late in 1869 and in the following year Berridge proceeded to England to pursue the matter.

He had also proceeded to England 17 years earlier to be trained, at his own expense, for the post of Lieutenant-Colonel of the St Kitts militia, and was quartered with the officers of the Brigade of Guards at Wellington Barracks. On returning to St Kitts, he threw himself heart and soul into everything connected with the militia.

On parade days, mounted on a magnificent curvetting bay, *Blink Bonnie*, a horse imported from America, Colonel Berridge was an unforgettable sight. He reorganised the militia and was eventually awarded the Long Service Medal in recognition of all he had done for the force.

During the visit to St Kitts in 1861 of Queen Victoria's second son, Prince Alfred, Probyn, as Aide de Camp, had much to do with the arrangements for his stay.

Eight years earlier, in 1843, he had got married in Fredericksted, St Croix. The marriage licence read:

> We, Christian the Eighth, by the Grace of God, King of Denmark, of the Vandals and Goths, Duke of Sleswick Holstein, Ditmark, Luanberg and Oldenburg, make known that We most graciously have permitted and allowed and do hereby permit and allow that Mr Thomas Probyn Berridge of St Kitts and Miss Maria Louisa Kortright Aarestrup of Our Island of St Croix in America, may without the previous publication of Banns from the Pulpit be married in the house, provided that there be no impediment to the lawful solemnisation of their union, but the Church and its Servants, the School, the Poor and those interested shall not be deprived of their due. UNDER OUR ROYAL SEAL.

The bride wore white satin embroidered with pearls and silver bugles, and the bridesmaids carried golden candlesticks with lighted candles. No record has survived of what the bridegroom wore.

The mystery of Christian William Aarestrup's mother
The bride's father was Major Christian William Aarestrup KD, the Collector of Customs Duties in Frederiksted, St Croix. In September 2002 I visited Copenhagen and found in the Danish National Archives a copy of his 1773 baptismal certificate.

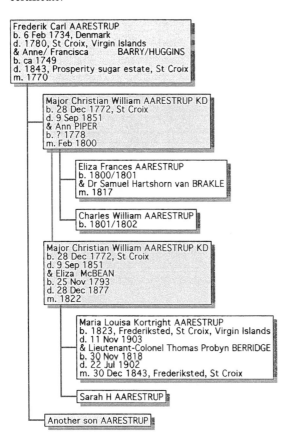

Frederik Carl AARESTRUP
b. 6 Feb 1734, Denmark
d. 1780, St Croix, Virgin Islands
& Anne/ Francisca   BARRY/HUGGINS
b. ca 1749
d. 1843, Prosperity sugar estate, St Croix
m. 1770

Major Christian William AARESTRUP KD
b. 28 Dec 1772, St Croix
d. 9 Sep 1851
& Ann PIPER
b. ? 1778
m. Feb 1800

Eliza Frances AARESTRUP
b. 1800/1801
& Dr Samuel Hartshorn van BRAKLE
m. 1817

Charles William AARESTRUP
b. 1801/1802

Major Christian William AARESTRUP KD
b. 28 Dec 1772, St Croix
d. 9 Sep 1851
& Eliza McBEAN
b. 25 Nov 1793
d. 28 Dec 1877
m. 1822

Maria Louisa Kortright AARESTRUP
b. 1823, Frederiksted, St Croix, Virgin Islands
d. 11 Nov 1903
& Lieutenant-Colonel Thomas Probyn BERRIDGE
b. 30 Nov 1818
d. 22 Jul 1902
m. 30 Dec 1843, Frederiksted, St Croix

Sarah H AARESTRUP

Another son AARESTRUP

And therein lies another of the little mysteries that occur in different parts of my family tree. The baptismal certificate is quite difficult to decipher, and it is of course in Danish, but it seems to state that Christian Wilhelm, the son of Frederik Carl Aarestrup and Francisca Huggins, was baptised on 10 January

1773 in Christiansted, St Croix. Francisca Huggins? Who is she? I have three versions of a document written in January 1913 by my great-grandmother, Alice Burt (nee Berridge), which is headed *According to Aunt Sarah Aarestrup*. (Aunt Sarah was Alice's aunt and Christian William Aarestrup's daughter.) According to this document, Christian William's mother was Anne Barry, a remarkable woman who was married four times.

Her story is worth telling. Anne was the daughter of Sir William Barry, the Governor of Antigua, 'and grand-daughter of Earl Fortescue'. She married at 15 a Captain Neville, 'a man of great wealth, a scion of the nobility'. But she did not love him. The marriage had been arranged by her parents.

A few months after the marriage, the young couple were thrown from their carriage, which Captain Neville had been driving. The young bride remained unconscious for several hours. Captain Neville was thought to be unhurt but, while watching by the side of his unconscious wife, he suddenly fell forward, blood gushing from mouth and ears, and in a few days he was dead.

Sixteen months later, Mrs Neville, a widow of great wealth and little more than 16, married her first love, her father's handsome secretary, Mr Locton. Eight months later Anne's second husband also met his death as a result of a sad accident. Inspecting a house under construction, which he planned to buy, he fell through the floor of an unfinished room and was so seriously injured that 'after a few hours of great agony, he expired'.

Some time later, Mrs Locton went to St Croix to visit Lady de Nully, a distant relative of her father, and there she met Frederik Carl Aarestrup, a theological student from Copenhagen who, owing to delicate health and a weak chest, was obliged to give up his studies and went out to St Croix as Government Secretary. In 1770 they got married. She was 21, and it was her third marriage.

And there was one more to come. Nearly two. Frederik died in 1780, and his widow married for a fourth time a Frenchman called Neve, 'who squandered her large property at a terrible rate, indulging in all sorts of extravagance and excesses. He lived for five or six years and, after his death, Mrs N was sought in marriage for the fifth time by a Captain Castonier, and she accepted him.

However, her two sons returned from school in Denmark at about this time and persuaded her to break off the engagement. She lived to be 94 'and was remarkable for the sweetness of her temper as well as for her exceeding beauty, a great part of which she retained to the close of her life'.

Also according to Aunt Sarah Aarestrup, "from the dear old lady the tureen and the punch bowl (the golden bowl) descended to its present owner the said Samuel William van Brakle, Chamberlain to His Majesty the King of Denmark". Samuel was her great-grandson and was indeed Chamberlain to the King from 1 January 1889 until his death just over 11 years later.

Curious to trace this golden bowl, when I was in Copenhagen in September

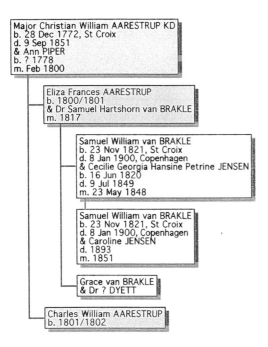

Major Christian William AARESTRUP KD
b. 28 Dec 1772, St Croix
d. 9 Sep 1851
& Ann PIPER
b. ? 1778
m. Feb 1800

Eliza Frances AARESTRUP
b. 1800/1801
& Dr Samuel Hartshorn van BRAKLE
m. 1817

Samuel William van BRAKLE
b. 23 Nov 1821, St Croix
d. 8 Jan 1900, Copenhagen
& Cecilie Georgia Hansine Petrine JENSEN
b. 16 Jun 1820
d. 9 Jul 1849
m. 23 May 1848

Samuel William van BRAKLE
b. 23 Nov 1821, St Croix
d. 8 Jan 1900, Copenhagen
& Caroline JENSEN
d. 1893
m. 1851

Grace van BRAKLE
& Dr ? DYETT

Charles William AARESTRUP
b. 1801/1802

2002, I visited the Landsarkivet for Sjaelland (the provincial archives for Zealand) and found that the Chamberlain had died intestate but the archives contained a long list of his effects at the time of his death. I took the list back to London and had it translated but, annoyingly, there was no mention of the golden bowl, although there was one blue and one red chamberlain's uniform with sword and hat worth 100 Kr -- a lot more than anything else on the long list.

So another, less important, mystery. Perhaps the golden bowl had been sold or given away before Samuel's death. But surely Aunt Sarah Aarestrup would have known the name of her own grandmother. And surely the baptismal certificate would not contain a gross error. I am mystified, although the certificate is almost illegible, and it is just possible that the Francisca Huggins mentioned was not the mother.

I have traced the Aarestrups back from Frederik Carl (born 1734), to his father Jens (born 1691), his grandfather Jacob (born 1664) and his great-grandfather Clemens, but I know nothing about them except their names and dates.

The mystery of James Samuel Berridge's sister-in-law

Another little mystery concerns Thomas Probyn Berridge's elder brother and the Master of Pembroke College, Cambridge. In 1953, when I was starting a

97

family of my own, Aunt Em wrote to me: "Your mother said you wanted to hear of some Berridge names" and she sent me a remarkable document written by Gladys Davis and entitled *Three Generations.*

It deals in the main with Gladys' parents, Benjamin Shuttleworth Davis and Annie Franziska Berridge, her grandparents Thomas Probyn Berridge and Maria Aarestrup, and her great-grandparents James Berridge and Alice Skinner. There is also quite a lot about Thomas' elder brother James Samuel Berridge, who became Treasurer of St Kitts and who sounds rather unpleasant. "Uncle James was very stuck up and Aunt Jane rather mean." "Unlike his genial younger brother, James was reserved and in his manner there was considerable hauteur....he held out two fingers to people he considered inferior."

I have also somehow acquired a handwritten document headed *Family Record* which seems to be Gladys' notes for *Three Generations.* There it says: "Uncle James went to Cambridge -- he married plain Jane Chapman, his cousin -- said to have proposed first to her pretty sister, who passed him on to Jane, while she married the Master of Pembroke, Dr Searle."

That seemed straightforward, but the name of the pretty sister was not given, and I was anxious to add her to the family tree, especially as she had married the Master of the college where my uncle, Bryan King, had spent 50 years of his life.

Charles Edward Searle was Master of Pembroke from 1880 to 1902 and before that Senior Tutor.

Until 1860 Cambridge dons were not allowed to marry. In that year the enforcement of celibacy was abolished by the University Commissioners but the colleges altered their own statutes as and when they wished. Unfortunately there is no mention of Dr Searle's marriage in the college archives, but the Pembroke parlour wine book provided an important clue.

On 4 January 1881 the Master gave a bottle of his own old Madeira 'quod bonum felix faustumque sit', that it may be good, happy and favourable, which is apparently the standard formula for marking an approaching marriage in the wine book. And against 7 February 1881 is written 'The prayer of January 4th having been fulfilled, the Master gave a bottle of wine on return from his Honey-moon'.

Armed with those dates, it was going to be a simple matter to find his marriage certificate at the Family Records Centre. But I should have smelt a rat at that stage. James Samuel Berridge married Jane Chapman on 20 April 1833. Is it likely that Jane's pretty sister would have rejected James in order to marry Dr Searle, then aged four, nearly 48 years later? Sure enough, his marriage certificate showed that his bride was a 30-year-old spinster called Mary Fowler, not Chapman. But, interestingly, the marriage was solemnised at the Church of St Edith in the Parish of Polesworth in the County of Warwick, which falls in the Registration District of Atherstone, where Jane Chapman lived.

I wondered if Dr Searle might have married twice, but this was indignantly denied by his grandson, the late Dr C W A Searle of Putney. "My grandfather did NOT [twice underlined] marry twice," he told me.

By the time the *Family Record* notes had become *Three Generations*, the story had changed slightly. Charles Searle had dropped out of the picture, Jane's surname is not mentioned, and her nameless pretty sister had become Mary. Instead we read: "Uncle James had been educated at the Charterhouse and at Trinity College [actually it was the much older Trinity Hall], Cambridge. He proposed to his pretty cousin, Mary, at Atherstone, but she refused him, saying 'Take Jane instead'. So he obediently married 'plain Jane', while she became the wife of Mr Scargill."

So how did Dr Searle get into the story in the first place? Polesworth, where Mary Fowler lived, is only four miles from Atherstone, where Jane Chapman lived. But their marriages were 48 years apart. How did the confusion arise? And who was Mr Scargill? All very puzzling.

Some years later I found out who Mr Scargill was. In the library of the Society of Genealogists I chanced upon a little document headed *Berridge Family Record. Saint Kitts, W.I. October 29.1890.* A note at the end says: "Written by Mr. Probyn Berridge, brother of James Samuel Berridge who married Jane, daur. of John Hood Chapman. This is copied from the original paper lent to me bt Mr. Robt. Power, April 1907. J.P.R."

I don't know who Mr Power was, but JPR was John Paul Rylands, the noted genealogist. Back, now, to Mr Scargill.

The family record written by Probyn starts with his great-great-grandfather John and John's two sons Matthew and Thomas and continues: "Matthew had a son named William (my grandfather) who married Elizabeth Hood, of Ashby de la Zouch, one of seven sisters; with her the name of Hood came into the family. Another of the seven sisters married Mr Chapman, father of John Hood Chapman, of Atherstone, Warwickshire; consequently she was the grandmother of my brother's wife -- & my father & John Hood Chapman first cousins."

After listing William's five sons, Probyn says that the sixth child, Elizabeth, "married Mr. Redford in Burton Crescent, her daughter Mary married John Scargill, a solicitor."

So both Jane Chapman and Mary Redford were second cousins to James Samuel Berridge. And the version in *Three Generations* of his rejected suit, where neither Jane's nor Mary's surname is mentioned and there is no suggestion that they are sisters, fully accords with Probyn's *Berridge Family Record*. But the mystery remains as to Dr Searle's connection with my family and how Mary Redford became confused with Mary Fowler.

The first Berridge in St Kitts
Like so many in this story, the father of Thomas Probyn and James Samuel

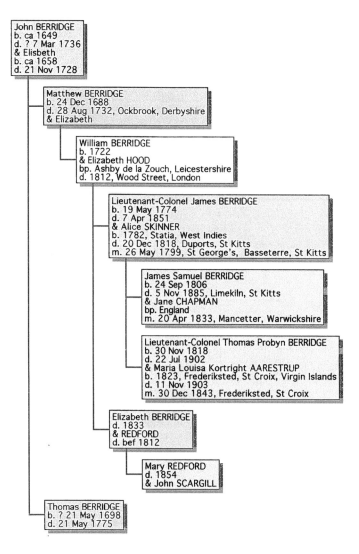

John BERRIDGE
b. ca 1649
d. ? 7 Mar 1736
& Elisbeth
b. ca 1658
d. 21 Nov 1728

Matthew BERRIDGE
b. 24 Dec 1688
d. 28 Aug 1732, Ockbrook, Derbyshire
& Elizabeth

William BERRIDGE
b. 1722
& Elizabeth HOOD
bp. Ashby de la Zouch, Leicestershire
d. 1812, Wood Street, London

Lieutenant-Colonel James BERRIDGE
b. 19 May 1774
d. 7 Apr 1851
& Alice SKINNER
b. 1782, Statia, West Indies
d. 20 Dec 1818, Duports, St Kitts
m. 26 May 1799, St George's, Basseterre, St Kitts

James Samuel BERRIDGE
b. 24 Sep 1806
d. 5 Nov 1885, Limekiln, St Kitts
& Jane CHAPMAN
bp. England
m. 20 Apr 1833, Mancetter, Warwickshire

Lieutenant-Colonel Thomas Probyn BERRIDGE
b. 30 Nov 1818
d. 22 Jul 1902
& Maria Louisa Kortright AARESTRUP
b. 1823, Frederiksted, St Croix, Virgin Islands
d. 11 Nov 1903
m. 30 Dec 1843, Frederiksted, St Croix

Elizabeth BERRIDGE
d. 1833
& REDFORD
d. bef 1812

Mary REDFORD
d. 1854
& John SCARGILL

Thomas BERRIDGE
b. ? 21 May 1698
d. 21 May 1775

Berridge, who was also called James, was something of an adventurer. We learn from his private letter book covering the years 1811 to 1821, extracts from which are quoted in *Three Generations*, that in 1794, when he was only 20, he went out from England to St Kitts 'with no resources but his own abilities'.

He eventually succeeded in setting up a mercantile business, the extent of which may be judged by allusions in his letters to the possession of several vessels 'trading through and among the islands and occasionally to Halifax and Bermuda or, in time of peace, to America'.

In addition to his business, he was Treasurer of St Kitts, Lieutenant-Colonel of the Windward Regiment of Foot and Aide de Camp to the Governor.

In 1799 he married the beautiful Alice Skinner, who was born on the neighbouring Dutch island of St Eustatius of Huguenot descent. She bore him seven children, dying, aged 36, just three weeks after the birth of Thomas Probyn. James wrote to a friend:

> I am sure you will be truly grieved at the contents of this letter and, knowing the goodness of your heart and the acuteness of your feelings, I consider it as a paramount duty to enveavour to suppress my own and to remind you that the All seeing Eye above directs we should bear with resignation the distress or afflictions He is pleased to burden us with, either in ourselves or our friends. We have never considered you or your brother in any other light than as a Brother and Sister, and I am sure I know and have always felt that your dear Father and Mother were like parents to me, and to mine, and I am sure you will, like a sister, feel for me and my dear, dear children when I inform you that I have forever lost my Beloved Alice, who departed this life of trouble and woe on Sunday evening at this place and was interred the same hour the following evening in the family vault in Basseterre ....

The large stone vault, with the Berridge arms (Argent, a saltier engrailed between four escallops sable) clearly discernible, still stands in St George's churchyard. James died in 1851 and, I imagine, joined his Beloved Alice in that vault.

Earlier Berridges
James had been one of a family of six. His eldest brother, Thomas, went to sea and drowned at Calcutta. The second son, William, was a crusty old lawyer in Hatton Garden, London, much given to criticising his brother James and his wife. William never married. The third son, John, also a lawyer, is equally critical of his sister-in-law.

In reply to John's complaints, James writes that Alice, being a West Indian, "a retinue of servants is one failing but, where she has one in England, she has at least four or five here. If I had a dozen children, there would be a dozen servants to attend them".

The fourth son was Robert. Like James, he went out to the West Indies. It seems that he married 'beneath him' in Martinique, had three daughters, and was 'such a trial to his relatives'.

Then came James, followed by Elizabeth, who married Mr Redford and whose daughter Mary married Mr Scargill.

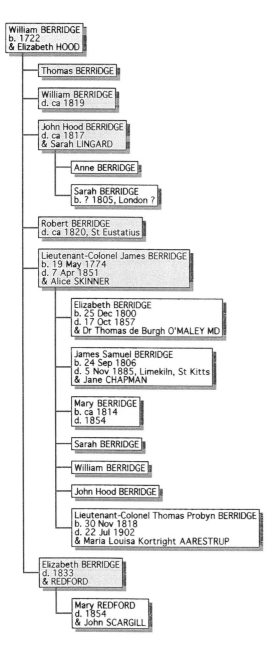

- **William BERRIDGE**
  b. 1722
  & Elizabeth HOOD
  - **Thomas BERRIDGE**
  - **William BERRIDGE**
    d. ca 1819
  - **John Hood BERRIDGE**
    d. ca 1817
    & Sarah LINGARD
    - **Anne BERRIDGE**
    - **Sarah BERRIDGE**
      b. ? 1805, London ?
  - **Robert BERRIDGE**
    d. ca 1820, St Eustatius
  - **Lieutenant-Colonel James BERRIDGE**
    b. 19 May 1774
    d. 7 Apr 1851
    & Alice SKINNER
    - **Elizabeth BERRIDGE**
      b. 25 Dec 1800
      d. 17 Oct 1857
      & Dr Thomas de Burgh O'MALEY MD
    - **James Samuel BERRIDGE**
      b. 24 Sep 1806
      d. 5 Nov 1885, Limekiln, St Kitts
      & Jane CHAPMAN
    - **Mary BERRIDGE**
      b. ca 1814
      d. 1854
    - **Sarah BERRIDGE**
    - **William BERRIDGE**
    - **John Hood BERRIDGE**
    - **Lieutenant-Colonel Thomas Probyn BERRIDGE**
      b. 30 Nov 1818
      d. 22 Jul 1902
      & Maria Louisa Kortright AARESTRUP
  - **Elizabeth BERRIDGE**
    d. 1833
    & REDFORD
    - **Mary REDFORD**
      d. 1854
      & John SCARGILL

I know nothing at all about James' father, William, except the names of his wife and six children. But I know that William's father, Matthew Berridge, was born on Christmas Eve 1688, died on 28 August 1732 at Ockbrook, Derbyshire, and was buried two days later at Kingston upon Soar, Nottinghamshire. And Matthew's father, John, was born at about the time that King Charles I was having his head chopped off in 1649 and died 87 years later in 1736. He too was buried at Kingston upon Soar.

That is as far back as I have got with the Berridges.

Chapter 12

'The ancient and illustrious House of Berkeley' and the Earle family

The man who turned into a clock,
Humphry Berkeley, homosexual law reformer, and the Cayon Diary

One of my middle names is Berkeley, as was my mother's. My great-grandfather Henry George King married Emily Verplank Bryan, the younger daughter of Charles and Mary Earle Bryan. Mrs Bryan was the daughter of Maurice Berkeley, whose father Henry is memorialised in St George's Church, Basseterre.

> This Tablet is erected by Thomas Berkeley Esqre of London to the Memory of his much respected father HENRY BERKELEY Esqre who was born in this island in January 1734 and was the son of Maurice Berkeley Esqre by Miss Tobin of Nevis -- Maurice Berkeley, descended from Maurice de Berkeley, one of the branches of the ancient and illustrious House of Berkeley of the County of Gloucester -- married in the year 1728 Miss Tobin, a daughter of the very respectable family of Tobin of the Island of Nevis and with his Lady came out to the West Indies where he did not long encounter the climate. He died leaving two sons Henry and Maurice. Henry was the father of seven sons and three daughters, of whom Thomas was the youngest of the sons. Maurice died unmarried. The high character for honor and integrity upheld in this colony by Henry Berkeley is universally acknowledged by all its inhabitants, and this humble memento is offered by his son as a tribute to his memory for having shown so virtuous an example to his posterity.

So that's no fewer than four Maurice Berkeleys in four generations. The first of them was born in 1661 and was admitted as a surgeon on 3 October 1692. He died in 1743 and was buried at St Saviour's, Southwark, which was then in Surrey but is now part of London.

The second Maurice was also a surgeon and seems to have been the first Berkeley to go out to the West Indies. Like his father, he was a surgeon and was paid £3 in St Kitts in 1732-3 'for attending coroner's inquest and opening a body'. His son was the Henry on the tablet in St George's. He was Provost Marshal of St Kitts for 30 years and, when he died in 1800, was worth between £7,000 and £8,000.

The third Maurice, Henry's elder brother, was a bachelor, and I don't know anything about him. The fourth Maurice lived in Martinique as well as St Kitts but died in 1804 in America, aged only 41. He had two daughters. The elder

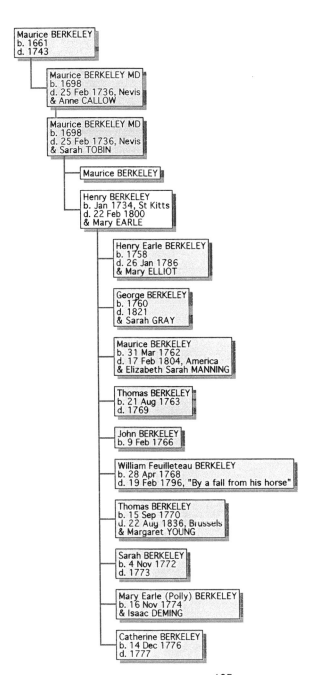

Maurice BERKELEY
b. 1661
d. 1743

Maurice BERKELEY MD
b. 1698
d. 25 Feb 1736, Nevis
& Anne CALLOW

Maurice BERKELEY MD
b. 1698
d. 25 Feb 1736, Nevis
& Sarah TOBIN

Maurice BERKELEY

Henry BERKELEY
b. Jan 1734, St Kitts
d. 22 Feb 1800
& Mary EARLE

Henry Earle BERKELEY
b. 1758
d. 26 Jan 1786
& Mary ELLIOT

George BERKELEY
b. 1760
d. 1821
& Sarah GRAY

Maurice BERKELEY
b. 31 Mar 1762
d. 17 Feb 1804, America
& Elizabeth Sarah MANNING

Thomas BERKELEY
b. 21 Aug 1763
d. 1769

John BERKELEY
b. 9 Feb 1766

William Feuilleteau BERKELEY
b. 28 Apr 1768
d. 19 Feb 1796, "By a fall from his horse"

Thomas BERKELEY
b. 15 Sep 1770
d. 22 Aug 1836, Brussels
& Margaret YOUNG

Sarah BERKELEY
b. 4 Nov 1772
d. 1773

Mary Earle (Polly) BERKELEY
b. 16 Nov 1774
& Isaac DEMING

Catherine BERKELEY
b. 14 Dec 1776
d. 1777

was my great-great-grandmother Mary Earle Berkeley, mentioned above, who constitutes my very tenuous link with Berkeley Castle in Gloucestershire. She married Charles Bryan. Her younger sister was Anne Howard, and her descendants are of interest.

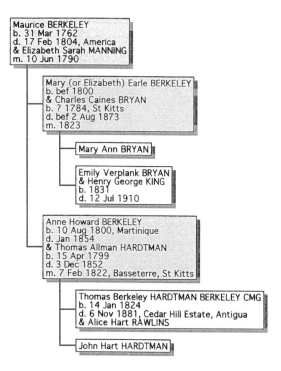

Maurice BERKELEY
b. 31 Mar 1762
d. 17 Feb 1804, America
& Elizabeth Sarah MANNING
m. 10 Jun 1790

Mary (or Elizabeth) Earle BERKELEY
b. bef 1800
& Charles Caines BRYAN
b. ? 1784, St Kitts
d. bef 2 Aug 1873
m. 1823

Mary Ann BRYAN

Emily Verplank BRYAN
& Henry George KING
b. 1831
d. 12 Jul 1910

Anne Howard BERKELEY
b. 10 Aug 1800, Martinique
d. Jan 1854
& Thomas Allman HARDTMAN
b. 15 Apr 1799
d. 3 Dec 1852
m. 7 Feb 1822, Basseterre, St Kitts

Thomas Berkeley HARDTMAN BERKELEY CMG
b. 14 Jan 1824
d. 6 Nov 1881, Cedar Hill Estate, Antigua
& Alice Hart RAWLINS

John Hart HARDTMAN

Anne Howard Berkeley married in 1822 Thomas Allman Hardtman, of whom I know nothing except for the dates of his birth (15 April 1799) and death (3 December 1852). But I know quite a lot about their son Thomas, who was born in 1824.

Like Pooh-Bah, his family pride was considerable. Although a Hardtman, he belonged to the 'ancient and illustrious House of Berkeley', and on the death of his mother in 1854 'with a view to perpetuate in his descendants his co-representation of his Maternal Grandfather' he assumed the surname of Berkeley in addition to that of Hardtman, becoming Thomas Berkeley Hardtman Berkeley.

This usage was given royal sanction, and the user is the only person in this family story to be memorialised by a large drinking fountain and clock. This impressive memorial dominates The Circus in Basseterre, built in the image of London's Piccadilly Circus but with a clock instead of Eros.

The memorial bears the following inscription:

This drinking fountain has been erected by the country men and private friends of The Late The Honourable Thomas Berkeley Hardtman Berkeley Companion of the Most Distinguished Order of St. Michael and St. George and President of the Legislative Council of the Leeward Islands, in recognition of the many valuable services he rendered this his Native Island as a Planter, a Politician and a Citizen. His Sterling qualities, his love of this Island and his deep interest in the welfare of the country at large entitle him to a Memorial by which his memory will be preserved and perpetuated. Born 14th January 1824. Died 6th December 1881.

One of Thomas Berkeley Hardtman Berkeley's grandsons was Captain Reginald Cheyne Berkeley MC, the playwright, Hollywood screenwriter and Liberal MP. He lost his seat in the House of Commons in 1924 and soon

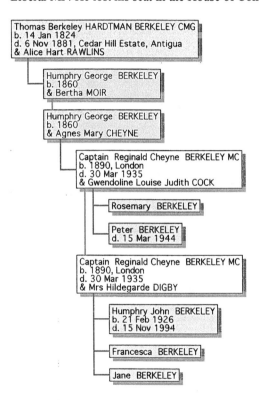

afterwards left his wife and ran away with and married his cook, Mrs Hildegarde Digby. Their first child, Humphry, born in 1926, made more of a mark on Parliament than had his father.

Humphry was Conservative MP for Lancaster from 1959 to 1966. He said later that in those seven years there were a number of issues on which he offended his party's tribal gods. He was in favour of rapidly granting independence to Britain's African's colonies and abstained from voting on the Commonwealth Immigrants Act of 1962 which, for the first time, limited the right of Commonwealth citizens to enter and freely settle in the UK.

He seconded Sidney Silverman's Bill which abolished capital punishment for murder. And he introduced into the Commons and obtained a second reading for the Sexual Offences Bill, under which homosexual acts committed in private by consenting male adults were no longer crimes.

He also spoke and voted in favour of the renunciation of peerages. For all these reasons I am proud to have know him and to have counted him a fourth cousin.

Undoubtedly it was his pioneering of homosexual law reform that cost him his parliamentary seat. The second reading of his Sexual Offences Bill took place just six weeks before polling day. The average national swing against the Conservatives was 3.5%; in Lancaster it was over 6%, and Humphry lost by nearly 2000 votes.

But it is his 'Berkeley memorandum' that will ensure his place in the political history books. In 1963, when the so-called 'magic circle' of Tory grandees secretly chose Sir Alec Douglas-Home as party leader, Humphry urged that Conservative MPs should be allowed to have a ballot, just as Labour MPs always have had. The new Tory leader asked Humphry to put his proposals in writing and then substantially adopted them in his own scheme for electing future party leaders.

Humphry wrote a number of books, the best of which "without question", according to his obituary in *The Times*, "was *The Life and Death of Rochester Sneath* (1974) -- the product of his contretemps with the authorities at Cambridge and in which, 25 years later, he revealed all the correspondence that had passed between himself -- posing as the headmaster of a minor public school called Selhurst -- and some of the most distinguished members of the Headmasters' Conference. It is a classic of its kind, easily outdoing in terms of hilarity anything later to be produced by Henry Root."

Humphry was at Pembroke College. When the hoax was discovered, the Master sent him down for two years, but he nevertheless obtained a degree and became President of the Union and Chairman of the Cambridge University Conservative Association.

I have a copy of his autobiography *Crossing the Floor*, inscribed 'For Chris & Betty with every good wish from Humphry'.

The Earle family
My mother's middle name was Berkeley; her brother Bryan's middle name was Earle. In fact these two family names crop up again and again. And the name

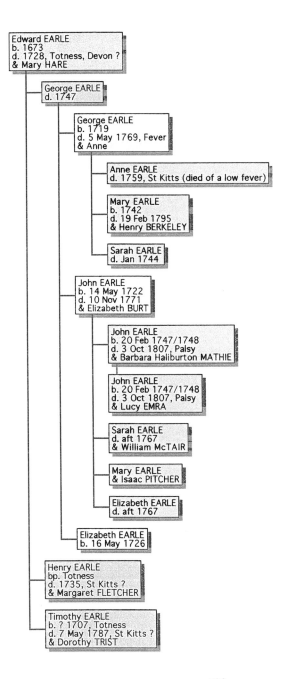

Edward EARLE
b. 1673
d. 1728, Totness, Devon ?
& Mary HARE

George EARLE
d. 1747

George EARLE
b. 1719
d. 5 May 1769, Fever
& Anne

Anne EARLE
d. 1759, St Kitts (died of a low fever)

Mary EARLE
b. 1742
d. 19 Feb 1795
& Henry BERKELEY

Sarah EARLE
d. Jan 1744

John EARLE
b. 14 May 1722
d. 10 Nov 1771
& Elizabeth BURT

John EARLE
b. 20 Feb 1747/1748
d. 3 Oct 1807, Palsy
& Barbara Haliburton MATHIE

John EARLE
b. 20 Feb 1747/1748
d. 3 Oct 1807, Palsy
& Lucy EMRA

Sarah EARLE
d. aft 1767
& William McTAIR

Mary EARLE
& Isaac PITCHER

Elizabeth EARLE
d. aft 1767

Elizabeth EARLE
b. 16 May 1726

Henry EARLE
bp. Totness
d. 1735, St Kitts ?
& Margaret FLETCHER

Timothy EARLE
b. ? 1707, Totness
d. 7 May 1787, St Kitts ?
& Dorothy TRIST

Berkeley occurs no less than eight times in John Earle's Cayon Diary. One of these entries records the death on 22 February 1800 of Henry Berkeley, "aged 66 and worth between 7 thousand and 8 thousand pounds". What the diary does not record is the fact that Henry Berkeley was the Provost Marshal of St Kitts and the husband of the diarist's first cousin Mary Earle. It might be appropriate for me to record here what I know of the Earles.

They were among the earliest settlers of St Kitts and Nevis. In 1672 Captain Roger Earle was a member of the Nevis House of Assembly, and in 1690 his son Colonel Edward Earle commanded a contingent of the Nevis militia and took part in the re-capture of the English quarter of St Kitts, which had been overrun by the French from their quarter of Basseterre.

Shortly after this, Edward's brother Samuel Earle became the proprietor of an estate in the parish of Cayon on the border of the English and French quarters. In 1705 the French again invaded and ravaged his plantation. However he recovered his fortunes and, after the final expulsion of the French from the island, he acquired a second estate, Laquerite, close to Basseterre. This estate remained in the possession of the Earles and was managed by them up to the end of the 19th century.

The Earles became connected to my family in 1745 when Elizabeth Burt married John Earle. Elizabeth was the daughter of Codrington Burt and Mary Bisse, and Codrington was the grandson of Colonel William Burt, the patriarch of the Burt family. When John died of apoplexy in 1771, he left his beloved wife £150, his chair carriage and the use of four of his negro slaves named Buster, Cob, Judy and Rose for the term of her natural life.

John Earle's ancestry is a little less certain. His father George, who died in 1747, may have been the son of Edward (1673-1728), who came from Totnes, or of Edward's brother Samuel. In any case John (1722-1771) was a sugar planter in Cayon as well as being a ship-owner. The first child of the Earle-Burt marriage was called John after his father, and it is his commonplace book, the Cayon Diary mentioned above, that is a rich source of information for the family histories of Kittitians and Nevisians.

From his youth, John junior kept careful notes about his relations and friends, and two years before his death he busied himself in puting more than a thousand of these notes, in his fine copperplate handwriting, in alphabetical order. These notes are mainly about births, marriages and deaths, but occasionally contemporary events are recorded.

John died of palsy in 1807, aged 60, and his death is noted in another hand. An attempt seems to have been made to continue the record, but it was soon abandoned. John Earle's records became incorporated with those of the two parishes of St Mary, Cayon, and Christ Church, Nicola Town, and were eventually bound with a register of Christ Church.

All these records were kept, and are still kept, at St Mary's rectory and in consequence became known as the Cayon Diary. In the 1960s they were tran-scribed by my late friend George Walker, a former Archdeacon of St Kitts, and my cousin Hazel Wigley (nee Walwyn). I am indebted to George for much of the above information.

But back to the Earles. As with so many West Indian families, the Earles are doubly connected to the Burts. John Earle who compiled the Cayon Diary had a sister Sarah who in 1785 married William McTair, and their daughter Eliza Anne McTair married George Henry Burt, my great-great-great-grandfather. So Eliza's grandmother was a Burt, and her husband was a Burt.

Diarist John married Barbara Haliburton Mathie in London in 1778 and brought his bride out to St Kitts the following year. Their first child, Mary Elizabeth, was born later that year, and a second daughter, Barbara Haliburton Margaret, was born two years later. The diary sadly records that the mother, the diarist's wife, died three weeks' later, aged 25 years, 10 months and 17 days.

Eight years later, John Earle married for a second time. His bride was Lucy Emra, the widow of another planter. Their son, Charles John Earle, was born on 28 June 1795 'Tuesday evening, 50 minutes past 9 o'clock' according to the diary.

Chapter 13

Three remarkable Burns brothers
and the Davis, Walwyn and Delisle families

*The philosopher, the colonial governor and the communist
and the families to which they are connected*

On the edge of my family tree, there are three distinguished, but very different, brothers. Their grandfather was Patrick Burns. He came from St Andrews in Scotland and was appointed Auditor of Antigua in 1870 and Auditor-General of the Leeward Islands in 1872. His salary in the latter post was £800 a year. Their father, James Burns, was Treasurer of St Kitts-Nevis and died in 1896 at the early age of 44.

The eldest of the three brothers was Cecil Delisle Burns. He took his middle name from his mother, Agnes Delisle, who was the daughter of the first of several Emile Delisles and, I think, the first Delisle in St Kitts.

Cecil Delisle Burns was born in 1879. He was educated at Christ's College, Cambridge, and in Rome, and was assistant secretary of the joint research department of the TUC and Labour Party from 1921 to 1924. He then became lecturer in logic and philosophy at Birkbeck College, London, from 1925 to 1927, and Stevenson Lecturer in Citizenship at Glasgow University from 1927 to 1936.

Twenty-one years earlier he had written a little book called *Political Ideals: Their Nature and Development*. I picked up a copy of it, beautifully printed and bound, for a shilling in George's Bookshop in Bristol in 1949.

Alan Burns was born in Basseterre eight years after Cecil and was sent, aged 12, to St Edmund's College, Ware, the oldest Catholic school in England. The family fortunes had been at a very low ebb since his father's death, so Alan did not go to university. Instead he joined the Treasury and Customs Department of St Kitts-Nevis in 1905, when he was 17.

He served in the Leeward Islands from 1905 to 1912 and in Nigeria from 1912 to 1924. He was then appointed Colonial Secretary of the Bahamas and spent five years there, acting as Governor on four occasions. In 1929 he went back to Nigeria as Deputy Chief Secretary for a further five years, before becoming Governor and Commander-in-Chief of British Honduras from 1934 to 1939.

By this time he was Sir Alan, having been made CMG in 1927 and KCMG in 1936. The GCMG was to follow in 1946.

At the beginning of the second world war he found himself at the Colonial Office as Assistant Under-Secretary of State. In 1941 he was sent to the Gold

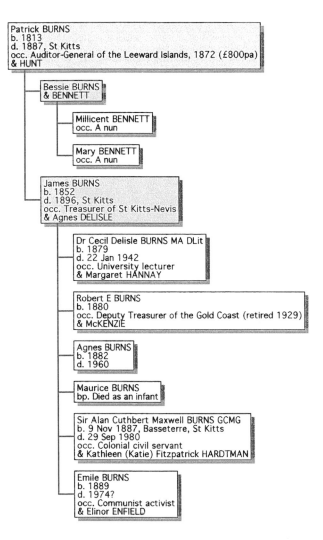

Patrick BURNS
b. 1813
d. 1887, St Kitts
occ. Auditor-General of the Leeward Islands, 1872 (£800pa)
& HUNT

Bessie BURNS
& BENNETT

Millicent BENNETT
occ. A nun

Mary BENNETT
occ. A nun

James BURNS
b. 1852
d. 1896, St Kitts
occ. Treasurer of St Kitts-Nevis
& Agnes DELISLE

Dr Cecil Delisle BURNS MA DLit
b. 1879
d. 22 Jan 1942
occ. University lecturer
& Margaret HANNAY

Robert E BURNS
b. 1880
occ. Deputy Treasurer of the Gold Coast (retired 1929)
& McKENZIE

Agnes BURNS
b. 1882
d. 1960

Maurice BURNS
bp. Died as an infant

Sir Alan Cuthbert Maxwell BURNS GCMG
b. 9 Nov 1887, Basseterre, St Kitts
d. 29 Sep 1980
occ. Colonial civil servant
& Kathleen (Katie) Fitzpatrick HARDTMAN

Emile BURNS
b. 1889
d. 1974?
occ. Communist activist
& Elinor ENFIELD

Coast as Governor and Commander in Chief until 1947, when he was appointed Permanent United Kingdom Representative on the Trusteeship Council of the United Nations, remaining at the UN until 1956.

Sir Alan wrote a number of books: *History of Nigeria; Colonial Civil Servant; Colour Prejudice;* and, most usefully from my point of view, *History of the British West Indies.* He died in 1980.

Sir Alan's younger brother Emile, who was born in 1889, followed a less conventional career and was for many years a leading member of the Commun-

113

ist Party of Great Britain. His name is not mentioned in his brother's autobiography.

Like Cecil but unlike Sir Alan, Emile did go to university. He went to Trinity College, Cambridge, but I don't know what he read. And I don't know what he did on leaving university. All I know is that by the end of the first world war he was a left-wing member of the Independent Labour Party, opposing its reformist leadership and demanding affiliation to the Third International.

In 1921 he joined the Communist Party, and by 1932 he was 'working closely with Pollitt' at the Communist Party's headquarters, according to my autographed copy of Noreen Branson's *History of the Communist Party of Great Britain 1927-1941*. He was also working closely with the London busmen's Rank and File Movement and editing their *Busmen's Punch*.

He had previously been general secretary of the Labour Research Department, an independent research body founded in 1912 by Beatrice Webb as part of the Fabian Society.

By 1935 Emile was head of the Communist Party's education and propaganda department. When in July 1936 a group of Spanish army officers, including General Franco, rebelled against the Republican government of Spain, an Aid-for-Spain movement developed in Britain in response to the Spanish government's appeal for medical supplies.

Soon individuals from many countries were joining units of the Republican army, and the Spanish government agreed to the formation of International Brigades. Harry Pollitt called for volunteers to go to Spain to help defend democracy, and by early January 1937 there were 450 Britons in Spain, and they formed the British Battalion of the International Brigade.

Later that month the Foreign Office declared that joining the Spanish forces was illegal under the Foreign Enlistment Act of 1870, but until then appeals for volunteers could be made quite openly in Britain, and those who wanted to go went to 16 King Street.

There they were seen by Emile Burns, Harry Pollitt, Palme Dutt and other leading Communists, who explained what would be expected of them and gave them tickets and money for the journey.

Eventually there were about 2,200 British International Brigaders. Many were wounded and maimed. Five hundred and twenty six were killed. Their example inspired the world.

When in September 1939 the British government declared war on Germany, the Communist Party backed the war but argued that fascism would not be defeated by the current Conservative government. It therefore called for a war on two fronts: against fascism and against the Chamberlain government.

But instructions for a total reversal of this policy soon arrived from the headquarters of the Communist International in Moscow. The Comintern was the international body whose decisions were binding on the national Communist parties. Its secretariat declared that the war was to be opposed as imperialist and unjust and that 'the division of states into fascist and democratic states has lost its former sense'.

For days the argument raged in the Central Committee of the British party, with Emile speaking passionately against the new line from Moscow and also against Palme Dutt's twisted arguments in its favour. According to Sam Aaronovitch, Emile hated Dutt. But in the end Emile voted, with considerable reservations, for the new policy.

Emile was a prolific writer and populariser of Marxism. Among his books and pamphlets were *Handbook of Marxism*, *What is Marxism?*, *The Only Way Out* and *Capitalism, Communism and the Transition*. During the second world war he edited the Communist Party's weekly paper *World News & Views*, and later on he edited the party's pale-blue-covered monthly, *Communist Review*.

Emile was first elected to the party's Central Committee in 1935 and remained a member of it for 22 years. He was also a member of its Political Bureau, or Political Committee as it was later called. His wife Elinor, a director of the London Co-operative Society, joined him on the Executive Committee in 1943 (the year it changed its name from Central Committee) and was re-elected several times.

At the party's 1947 congress, much stress was laid on the need to develop the party's ideological work, and a Cultural Committee was set up with Emile in the chair. According to the poet Arnold Rattenbury, Emile was seen as a 'very on the party line' comrade by almost all of the party's writers and historians and was greatly loathed by them. The historian Eric Hobsbawm says that he was bureaucratic and a bit impersonal.

On the other hand, George Matthews, a former editor of the *Daily Worker*, says that Emile was the nicest party leader he ever knew. "I was very fond of him and Elinor. Harry Pollitt once said to me that Emile told him that he and Elinor had never exchanged a cross word. I would have found this very difficult to believe of any other couple, but not of those two."

After my wife Betty and I returned from Budapest to London, perhaps in 1957 or 1958, Emile came and had dinner with us at our home in Holland Road, Kensington. I remember that he seemed very old and was somewhat deaf. And there was one further meeting. My diary for Wednesday 12 August 1959 says simply '1.45 Emile Burns'. But I have no idea what that was about.

There were two more brothers and one sister. Robert was born in 1880, Maurice died in infancy, and Agnes was born in 1882 and died in 1960. I know nothing else about them.

As already mentioned, their mother, before she married James Burns, was Agnes Delisle. Agnes' sister Marie married John Wentworth Thurston, a much respected local figure in Basseterre and founder of the firm J W Thurston. And

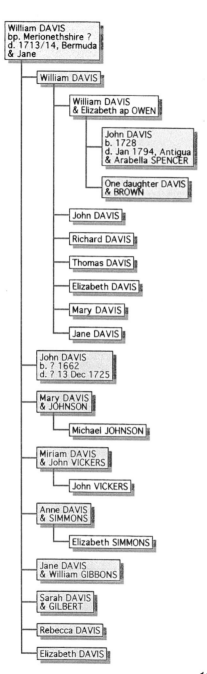

William DAVIS
bp. Merionethshire ?
d. 1713/14, Bermuda
& Jane

William DAVIS

William DAVIS
& Elizabeth ap OWEN

John DAVIS
b. 1728
d. Jan 1794, Antigua
& Arabella SPENCER

One daughter DAVIS
& BROWN

John DAVIS

Richard DAVIS

Thomas DAVIS

Elizabeth DAVIS

Mary DAVIS

Jane DAVIS

John DAVIS
b. ? 1662
d. ? 13 Dec 1725

Mary DAVIS
& JOHNSON

Michael JOHNSON

Miriam DAVIS
& John VICKERS

John VICKERS

Anne DAVIS
& SIMMONS

Elizabeth SIMMONS

Jane DAVIS
& William GIBBONS

Sarah DAVIS
& GILBERT

Rebecca DAVIS

Elizabeth DAVIS

their daughter Ismee married Geoffrey (later Sir Geoffrey) Boon and ran the first school I attended as a little boy. And Geoffrey Boon's first cousin Beatrice married my grandmother's youngest brother, Edmund, founder of the Canadian Burt dynasty.

Agnes Burns' youngest brother Gustave was the father of Kathleen Delisle, who married Basil Davis, who was manager of the St Kitts (Basseterre) Sugar Factory when I was a child. Basil was the youngest son of Benjamin Shuttleworth Davis and Annie Franziska Berridge, who was the daughter of Thomas Probyn Berridge and Maria Louisa Kortright Aarestrup, whom we encountered in Chapter 11.

Basil Davis' youngest daughter Terry married Christopher Desmond Elliott Walwyn, my second cousin not just once but twice. His grandfather, Charles Lloyd Walwyn had married first my grandfather's sister, Mary Berkeley King, and then my grandmother's sister, Adeline Hamilton Burt.

Thus were the white families on the small island of St Kitts connected and re-connected over and over again.

The Davis family
William Davis emigrated from Merionethshire and settled in Bermuda sometime in the 17th century. He had nine children and died in 1713 or 1714. One of his children was called John, and he might have been the Colonel John Davis who was 'President of His Majesty's Council of the Island of St Christophers, who died the 13th of December 1725 Aged 63 Years' and was buried in the south nave aisle of Westminster Abbey.

I have been unable to prove the connection but the dates seem right. There is now no trace of his grave just east of the west cloister door, but his memorial survives, although it has been moved to the first bay of the north nave aisle. It consists of a white marble mural tablet, in the form of a curtain with a gilded fringe, surmounted by a cartouche of arms.

William Davis' eldest son and his eldest grandson were also called William. Grandson William settled in Antigua in 1728, and his son John was born the same year. When John died 66 years later, he owned the Hawes and Cocoa Nut Hall sugar plantations on the island. John's son, Benjamin Brown Davis, was also a planter. He left Antigua for St Kitts in 1806 and owned Belmont estate. He was a member of the Council of St Kitts and could therefore stick Honourable in front of his name, but it seems that he was a spendthrift and ran up huge debts.

Benjamin's eldest son, William Darnell Davis, became Chief Justice of Grenada. His second son, John Nicholas, died in infancy. His third son, Steuart Spencer Davis, inherited Belmont estate, and married Anna Louisa Burt, Archibald Paull's youngest sister. Steuart is said to have been a good planter and was also thrifty. In 11 years he paid off the debt of about £11,000.

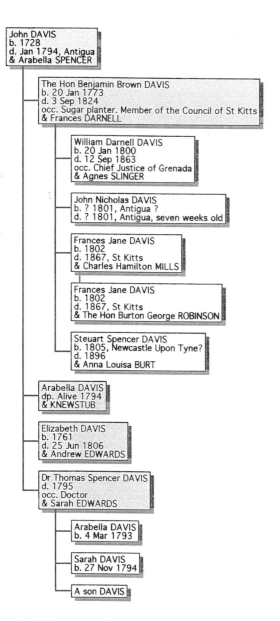

John DAVIS
b. 1728
d. Jan 1794, Antigua
& Arabella SPENCER

The Hon Benjamin Brown DAVIS
b. 20 Jan 1773
d. 3 Sep 1824
occ. Sugar planter. Member of the Council of St Kitts
& Frances DARNELL

William Darnell DAVIS
b. 20 Jan 1800
d. 12 Sep 1863
occ. Chief Justice of Grenada
& Agnes SLINGER

John Nicholas DAVIS
b. ? 1801, Antigua ?
d. ? 1801, Antigua, seven weeks old

Frances Jane DAVIS
b. 1802
d. 1867, St Kitts
& Charles Hamilton MILLS

Frances Jane DAVIS
b. 1802
d. 1867, St Kitts
& The Hon Burton George ROBINSON

Steuart Spencer DAVIS
b. 1805, Newcastle Upon Tyne?
d. 1896
& Anna Louisa BURT

Arabella DAVIS
dp. Alive 1794
& KNEWSTUB

Elizabeth DAVIS
b. 1761
d. 25 Jun 1806
& Andrew EDWARDS

Dr Thomas Spencer DAVIS
d. 1795
occ. Doctor
& Sarah EDWARDS

Arabella DAVIS
b. 4 Mar 1793

Sarah DAVIS
b. 27 Nov 1794

A son DAVIS

In 1876 he retired to Bournemouth. When he died, aged 91, he left £20,000 to each of his four daughters. His eldest son was Benjamin Shuttleworth Davis. It is said that he liked Latin and Greek and did not like being a planter,

118

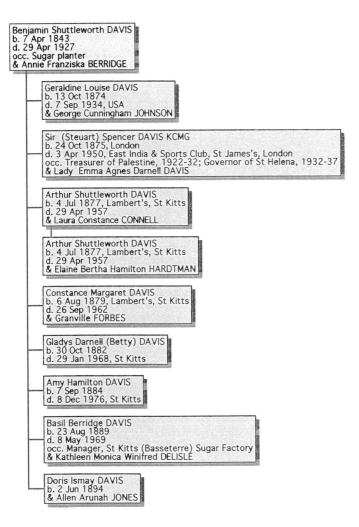

Benjamin Shuttleworth DAVIS
b. 7 Apr 1843
d. 29 Apr 1927
occ. Sugar planter
& Annie Franziska BERRIDGE

Geraldine Louise DAVIS
b. 13 Oct 1874
d. 7 Sep 1934, USA
& George Cunningham JOHNSON

Sir (Steuart) Spencer DAVIS KCMG
b. 24 Oct 1875, London
d. 3 Apr 1950, East India & Sports Club, St James's, London
occ. Treasurer of Palestine, 1922-32; Governor of St Helena, 1932-37
& Lady Emma Agnes Darnell DAVIS

Arthur Shuttleworth DAVIS
b. 4 Jul 1877, Lambert's, St Kitts
d. 29 Apr 1957
& Laura Constance CONNELL

Arthur Shuttleworth DAVIS
b. 4 Jul 1877, Lambert's, St Kitts
d. 29 Apr 1957
& Elaine Bertha Hamilton HARDTMAN

Constance Margaret DAVIS
b. 6 Aug 1879, Lambert's, St Kitts
d. 26 Sep 1962
& Granville FORBES

Gladys Darnell (Betty) DAVIS
b. 30 Oct 1882
d. 29 Jan 1968, St Kitts

Amy Hamilton DAVIS
b. 7 Sep 1884
d. 8 Dec 1976, St Kitts

Basil Berridge DAVIS
b. 23 Aug 1889
d. 8 May 1969
occ. Manager, St Kitts (Basseterre) Sugar Factory
& Kathleen Monica Winifred DELISLE

Doris Ismay DAVIS
b. 2 Jun 1894
& Allen Arunah JONES

although he owned and managed Belmont, Saddler's and Lambert's estates in
St Kitts. He married Annie Franziska Berridge. They had eight children.

Their eldest son, with the same names as his grandfather, Steuart Spencer
Davis, like so many in this story, was a distinguished colonial civil servant. He
wrote the mandate for Palestine and was its Treasurer from 1922 to 1932.

He was knighted in 1930 and was Governor of St Helena from 1932 to 1937.
Sir Spencer Davis died, aged 74, in 1950 at the East India and Sports Club in
St James's, London.

He had married his second cousin Emma Agnes Darnell Davis in 1915. She died in 1946, leaving a net estate of £16,637 9s 4d. Sir Spencer's net estate was worth £62 17s.

One day in 2001 I received out of the blue an email from someone who had learnt from the St Kitts-Nevis genealogy website that I was researching the Davis family. She wanted to know if I could tell her anything about Steuart Darnell Spencer Davis. I said: yes, his father was Steuart Spencer Davis, his grandfather was Benjamin Shuttleworth Davis, his great-grandfather was Steuart Spencer Davis and his great-great-grandfather was Benjamin Brown Davis, but I don't really know anything more about Steuart Darnell Spencer Davis himself.

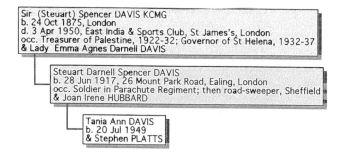

Sir (Steuart) Spencer DAVIS KCMG
b. 24 Oct 1875, London
d. 3 Apr 1950, East India & Sports Club, St James's, London
occ. Treasurer of Palestine, 1922-32; Governor of St Helena, 1932-37
& Lady Emma Agnes Darnell DAVIS

Steuart Darnell Spencer DAVIS
b. 28 Jun 1917, 26 Mount Park Road, Ealing, London
occ. Soldier in Parachute Regiment; then road-sweeper, Sheffield
& Joan Irene HUBBARD

Tania Ann DAVIS
b. 20 Jul 1949
& Stephen PLATTS

Amazingly it turned out that my correspondent was his daughter, who hadn't seen him or heard from him since she was a little girl.Her last contact was a letter dated 'Sat. 6th. Dec' written probably in 1958 from Simpson's-in-the-Strand. According to Tania, for that was her name, her father had been an officer in the Coldstream Guards or the Royal Horse Guards in the second world war and had been wounded three times.

In a letter to Tania from Toronto, the late Steuart Arthur Hamilton Davis said that her father, his first cousin, was in the Coldstream Guards and was commissioned. But his name does not appear in the Army Lists for the period of the second world war, which indicates that he did not hold a commission.

Tania later discovered that he had been a private in the Parachute Regiment and was in 11 Platoon, 'B' Coy, in the 9th Parachute Battalion in Holland, near Roermond on the Maas, and that his sergeant's name was Michael Corboy.

Her mother had married Steuart in Sheffield in 1944 after a six-week whirl-wind romance but he had a serious argument with his father and they did not speak. He did not even tell his father of Tania's birth in 1949.

Steuart Darnell Spencer Davis had inherited £23,000 from his mother and grandmother but he became estranged from his wife and, convinced that she was after his money, he ran through £8,000 in eight months in order to deprive her of alimony. He took a job as a road-sweeper with Sheffield Borough Council, earning £4 18s a week and went up to London at the weekends to squander his fortune in riotous living. He was brought before the Sheffield magistrates in 1953 for failing to pay his wife £43 5s maintenance arrears. He was supposed to pay her £2 a week plus 30s for his daughter. He was last heard of in a hospital near St Albans, which has since closed down.

Both Tania and I, separately, have tried very hard to trace him, using the Family Tracing Service of the Salvation Army, the General Register Office's Traceline and even a private detective, but without success. My letter from the Salvation Army said: "Steuart's carer did get in touch with this office, on Steuart's behalf, and indicated that contact is not desired at this time". Sad.

Benjamin Shuttleworh Davis died in 1927, just a year before I was born, but I remember being taken regularly as a child to see his widow, Annie, then in her 80s, who was always At Home at Greenways on Sunday afternoons. She was my great-grandmother's youngest sister and eight years her junior.

With Aunt Annie Davis at Greenways all those Sunday afternoons ago were her two unmarried daughters, Aunt Gladys and Aunt Amy. Gladys changed her name, I don't know why, to Betty and wrote *Three Generations*, an account of the lives and times of her parents, grandparents and great-grandparents, starting with James and Alice Berridge, who were her great-grandparents and my great-great-great-grandparents. She lived to be 85. Her younger sister Amy lived to be 92.

Their older brother Arthur Shuttleworth Davis married twice. His first wife, Laura Constance Connell, gave him two daughters, one of whom, Gwen, married William Stedman Archer -- all the male Archers seem to have Stedman as a second name. Gwen was a friend of my mother, and as a child I knew both the Archer children, David and Marian. David and his father both died before they were 50 -- in marked contrast to the long-lived Davises.

Arthur's second wife was Elaine Bertha Hamilton Hardtman, who must, I think, have been related, but I don't know how, to Thomas Berkeley Hardtman Berkeley, memorialised by the Circus clock in Basseterre. Elaine had three sons. Robert died in infancy but Steuart and William lived to be 87 and 74 respectively. Their father Arthur was one of a contingent of four from the St Kitts Volunteer Force at the coronation of King George V in 1910 and died, aged 79 in 1957.

The Davises not only lived long, they also attended coronations. Arthur's father Benjamin represented St Kitts at the 1910 coronation, and Arthur's younger brother Basil did the same at the 1937 coronation of King George VI. Benjamin was 84 when he died; Basil was 79.

Benjamin and Annie's fourth child was Constance Margaret, who, like a good Davis, lived to be 83. When she was 26, she married, at Lambert's in St Kitts, Granville Forbes from Scotland. According to family lore, he kissed the Queen Mother at a dance at the Castle of Mey when she was still Lady Elizabeth Bowes-Lyon.

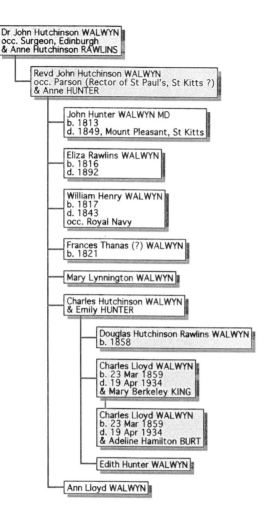

Dr John Hutchinson WALWYN
occ. Surgeon, Edinburgh
& Anne Hutchinson RAWLINS

Revd John Hutchinson WALWYN
occ. Parson (Rector of St Paul's, St Kitts ?)
& Anne HUNTER

John Hunter WALWYN MD
b. 1813
d. 1849, Mount Pleasant, St Kitts

Eliza Rawlins WALWYN
b. 1816
d. 1892

William Henry WALWYN
b. 1817
d. 1843
occ. Royal Navy

Frances Thanas (?) WALWYN
b. 1821

Mary Lynnington WALWYN

Charles Hutchinson WALWYN
& Emily HUNTER

Douglas Hutchinson Rawlins WALWYN
b. 1858

Charles Lloyd WALWYN
b. 23 Mar 1859
d. 19 Apr 1934
& Mary Berkeley KING

Charles Lloyd WALWYN
b. 23 Mar 1859
d. 19 Apr 1934
& Adeline Hamilton BURT

Edith Hunter WALWYN

Ann Lloyd WALWYN

Their son was Sir Alastair Forbes. He was a judge and was President of the Courts of Appeal for St Helena, the Falklands and British Antartica from 1965 to 1988.

I've already mentioned Gladys and Amy Davis. The seventh child, Basil, was Manager of the St Kitts (Basseterre) Sugar Factory when I was a child, and I grew up with his children, Pam, Jill, Terry and Tony. A photograph of Mrs Boon's pupils taken early in the 1930s shows Pam in the second row and Jill, Terry, my cousin Chris Walwyn and me in the front. Terry was my first girl friend, but she married the other Chris. The youngest of the Davis children, Tony, is not in the photograph. He wasn't born until 1931.

Being manager of the sugar factory put one pretty high up the social scale in the St Kitts of the 1930s, and Basil and Kathleen and their children lived in a large and lovely house near the factory. I was privileged to swim with them in the biggest and best swimming-pool on the island, filled with the cooling waters from the factory.

Benjamin and Annie's eighth child, Doris, married an American, Allen Aruna Jones, and they had a son, Richard Basil, whom I knew as Dickie in London in the early 1950s, when he was working as a supply teacher, taking singing lessons and learning Russian.

The Walwyn family

As I said, Terry Davis married my cousin Chris Walwyn. His family can be traced back to Thomas Walwin or Walwyn who was living in Nevis in 1677 with his wife, four sons, two daughters and a numbert of slaves. Thomas had a son called John, who died in 1757, and John had a son called William who married Anne Hutchinson Lynnington, a niece of Dr John Hutchinson and a sister of Elizabeth, Joseph Rawlins' wife.

These names -- Rawlins, Hutchinson, Lynnington -- crop up again and again. Henry Rawlins, born in 1695, lived in Nicola Town, St Kitts. Benjamin Hutchinson married Anne Mathew Burt, one of the daughters of Colonel William Pym Burt, the Chief Justice and Treasurer of St Kitts. At least four Walwyns were given Lynnington as a second name. But I digress.

William and Anne Walwyn's eldest son was Dr John Hutchinson Walwyn, a surgeon in Edinburgh, and he married his first cousin Anne Rawlins, the daughter of Joseph and Elizabeth Rawlins. The surgeon's elder son was called John Hutchinson after his father and became a clergyman. The surgeon's younger son, Joseph Rawlins Walwyn (you see what I mean about these names croping up again and again and again) died in 1808, aged 19, of yellow fever with his regiment in Surinam.

Four years later, his elder brother, the Revd John Hutchinson Walwyn, married Anne Hunter of Knapton in Norfolk. They had seven children. Their eldest, John Hunter Walwyn, died, aged 36, after falling from his horse at Mount Pleasant in St Kitts. Their youngest, Charles Hutchinson Walwyn, married his first cousin Emily Hunter in 1856 in England.

And it was Charles and Emily's son, Charles Lloyd Walwyn, who first married my grandfather's sister and then, after her death, married my grandmother's sister.

The eldest of the three children of Charles Lloyd Walwyn and his first wife, Mary Berkeley King, was William Earle Llewellyn Walwyn, know as Willie. Willie outdid his father by marrying three times and by fathering his seventh child just before he died, aged 69, in 1954.

Charles' second wife was Adeline Hamilton Burt, Aunt Addie to me, and

Charles Lloyd WALWYN
b. 23 Mar 1859
d. 19 Apr 1934
& Mary Berkeley KING

William Earle Llewellyn WALWYN
b. Sep 1884
d. 1954
occ. Sugar estates manager
& Gertrude BRAND

Lt-Colonel Charles Earle Berkeley WALWYN DSO OBE
b. 7 Dec 1913
occ. Soldier, Lt-Colonel in the Grenadier Guards
& Enid PAVÉ

Kathleen Mary Berkeley WALWYN
b. 15 Dec 1921
& Bruce Gordon WIGGINS

Kathleen Mary Berkeley WALWYN
b. 15 Dec 1921
& Henry HOWARD

Hazel Angela Savery WALWYN
& Captain John Leslie (Jack) WIGLEY

Keith Lynnington WALWYN
b. 25 May 1924, Douglas Estate, St Kitts
d. 15 Dec 1938, Aldenham School, Herts, England

Christopher Desmond Elliott WALWYN MBE
b. 16 Jan 1926, St Kitts
& Kathleen Doris Therese DAVIS

Christopher Desmond Elliott WALWYN MBE
b. 16 Jan 1926, St Kitts
& Joy

William Earle Llewellyn WALWYN
b. Sep 1884
d. 1954
occ. Sugar estates manager
& Helen Marjorie Berkeley HARDTMAN

William Earle Llewellyn WALWYN
b. Sep 1884
d. 1954
occ. Sugar estates manager
& Mary HAMMOND

Howard WALWYN
b. 1953
occ. Dealer in antique clocks

Charlotte WALWYN
b. 1954

Emily Linnington WALWYN
& ? WYNNE

Howard Hutchinson WALWYN
& Evelyn LEVEROCK

124

they had five children. I knew the two yougest, Daphne and Douglas. Daphne married Teddy Boyce, who, like my father, worked for Barclays (DC&O). They had two boys, Michael and Timothy, and I was Timothy's godfather.

Douglas, 12 older than me, boarded with Aunty and Aunt Em in Cayon Street, Basseterre, when I was a child. He fought in the second world war, read law and worked as a magistrate in Jamaica afterwards, dying there, aged only 44, in 1961.

Let us return to Willie Walwyn. He manged various sugar estates in St Kitts, notably, when I was a child, Douglas, just north of Basseterre, and later Estridge in the parish of Christ Church, Nicola Town. His first wife, whom I remember well, was Gertrude Brand, known as Gertie, and they had five children.

Their eldest, Charles Earle Berkeley Walwyn, born in 1913, went to the Royal Military College, Sandhurst, and then into the Gloucestershire Regiment. He was commissioned as a Second Lieutenant in 1934, made Lieutenant in 1937 and Captain in 1942. He had the temporary rank of Lieutenant-Colonel in the second world war and was awarded the DSO. He fought with the Glosters in the Korean war and was made a proper Lieutenant-Colonel in 1954. Three years later he was awarded the OBE. He married Enid Pave, and spent his retirement in St Kitts. They had three children, of whom I only know the youngest, Philip.

Willie and Gertie's second child, born in 1921, was Kathleen Mary Berkeley Walwyn, known as Berkeley, which we pronounced Burkley rather than Barkley, or Berks, pronounced Burks. After the second world war, Berks married Bruce Wiggins, a paralysed war veteran.

Bruce was the grandson of my grandmother's elder sister, Ingeborg Mabel Burt, so he was my second cousin. And Berks was the granddaughter of my grandfather's younger sister, so she was also my second cousin.

Bruce joined the Canadian army when war broke out and took a bullet in the spine, which paralysed him from the waist down, so Berks did a very brave and selfless thing when she married him but, sadly, their marriage ended in divorce, and Berks married Henry Howard, who had been Administrator of St Kitts.

Berks' younger sister Hazel, or Hazel Angela Savery Walwyn to give her names in full, married Jack Wigley, whose great-great-grandfather, George Henry Burt, was my great-great-great-grandfather. There were two more boys after Hazel. Keith Lynnington Walwyn, always know as Lynn, was born in 1924, and his parents sent him to school in England, where he joined my uncle Harry at Aldenham. Lynn was with us for our large family holiday at Seaview in the Isle of Wight in the summer of 1938. In December he developed a brain tumour and died after an unsuccessful operation. He was only 14.

Chris Walwyn was nearly two years younger than Lynn. He went to the

Antigua Grammar School and then to London to read law. When I arrived in London from Barbados in September 1946, Chris was already there, and I spent my first few days with him at his boarding house in Earl's Court before going on to Bristol. It seems that his full name was Christopher Desmond Elliott Walwyn, although Chris himself always thought it was Christopher Elliott Desmond. What is beyond doubt is that he was awarded an MBE to place after his surname for his work for the St Kitts sugar industry.

As already mentioned, Chris married Terry Davis, and they had three children, but the marriage did not last. Chris' second wife, a lovely lady from Trinidad, is called Joy.

Chris' mother, Gertie, died just after the war, and Willie married, in 1947, Marjorie Holmes a Court, the widow of Leonard Wyndham Daly Holmes a Court MBE. Before her first marriage, Marjorie had been Helen Marjorie Berkeley Hardtman. You can see how the same St Kitts names come round again and again.

After Marjorie died, Willie married again. His third wife was Mary Hammond, and they had two children. Howard was born in 1953, and Charlotte in 1954. Her father died the same year, aged 69, some weeks before his daughter was born.

The Delisle family

According to Sir Probyn Inniss' *Historic Basseterre*, the biggest shipping and general merchant in the town in the 1850s was Emile Delisle. This Emile Delisle was the son of Emile Sapenne Delisle, who was, I think, the first Delisle on the island. His parents were Antoine Delisle and Zulma Perrillier.

Emile Sapenne Delisle's wife was Agnes Sapenne Cock; the fact that both had the middle name Sapenne suggests that they were not unrelated. Their son Emile, the shipper and general merchant, was in fact Emile S Delisle, and I strongly suspect that the S stood for Sapenne.

There are more Sapennes to come. Emile S's brother was Gustave Sapenne Delisle, and Gustave's son, yet another Emile Sapenne Delisle, was running the family firm when I was a little boy in Basseterre. One of Gustave's sisters rejoiced in the name of Marie Margerite Rosatie Sapenne Delisle, and she married John Wentworth Thurston, a much respected local figure of 'mixed blood'. The Delisle family approved of the match (and in those days not everyone would have done), and Marie's brother Emile, the founder of the shipping and general merchant's firm, produced £5,000 as a sort of dowry to set them up.

Thurston was an employee of Wade and Abbott, a firm which combined sugar production and merchandising, a highly profitable combination. When Samuel J Abbott retired in 1900, Thurston took over the firm, setting up his own company J W Thurston & Co Ltd, with trading interests including

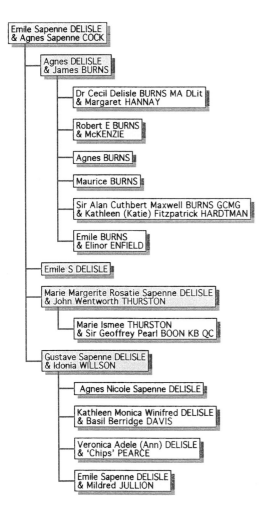

Emile Sapenne DELISLE & Agnes Sapenne COCK

　Agnes DELISLE & James BURNS

　　　Dr Cecil Delisle BURNS MA DLit & Margaret HANNAY

　　　Robert E BURNS & McKENZIE

　　　Agnes BURNS

　　　Maurice BURNS

　　　Sir Alan Cuthbert Maxwell BURNS GCMG & Kathleen (Katie) Fitzpatrick HARDTMAN

　　　Emile BURNS & Elinor ENFIELD

　Emile S DELISLE

　Marie Margerite Rosatie Sapenne DELISLE & John Wentworth THURSTON

　　　Marie Ismee THURSTON & Sir Geoffrey Pearl BOON KB QC

　Gustave Sapenne DELISLE & Idonia WILLSON

　　　Agnes Nicole Sapenne DELISLE

　　　Kathleen Monica Winifred DELISLE & Basil Berridge DAVIS

　　　Veronica Adele (Ann) DELISLE & 'Chips' PEARCE

　　　Emile Sapenne DELISLE & Mildred JULLION

shipping, insurance and estate supplies. In 1974 the St Kitts-Nevis-Anguilla Trading and Development Co Ltd (TDC) acquired the assets of Thurston's and became the largest company of its kind in the state.

John Wentworth and Marie Thurston had three children, one of whom was the 'Miss Ismee', later Lady Boon, who ran the old-fashioned dame school that I attended as a small boy. And J W Thurston's younger brother Allan Otty Thurston married my grandfather's sister, Annie Earle King, known to us all as 'Miss Annie'.

Back to the Delisles. Gustave's eldest sister Agnes we have already met as the wife of James Burns, the Treasurer of St Kitts-Nevis, and the mother of the

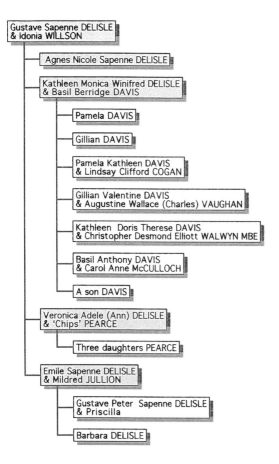

Gustave Sapenne DELISLE
& Idonia WILLSON
├─ Agnes Nicole Sapenne DELISLE
├─ Kathleen Monica Winifred DELISLE
│   & Basil Berridge DAVIS
│   ├─ Pamela DAVIS
│   ├─ Gillian DAVIS
│   ├─ Pamela Kathleen DAVIS
│   │   & Lindsay Clifford COGAN
│   ├─ Gillian Valentine DAVIS
│   │   & Augustine Wallace (Charles) VAUGHAN
│   ├─ Kathleen Doris Therese DAVIS
│   │   & Christopher Desmond Elliott WALWYN MBE
│   ├─ Basil Anthony DAVIS
│   │   & Carol Anne McCULLOCH
│   └─ A son DAVIS
├─ Veronica Adele (Ann) DELISLE
│   & 'Chips' PEARCE
│   └─ Three daughters PEARCE
└─ Emile Sapenne DELISLE
    & Mildred JULLION
        ├─ Gustave Peter Sapenne DELISLE
        │   & Priscilla
        └─ Barbara DELISLE

three remarkable Burns brothers. Gustave married Idonia Willson, and they had four children. The eldest, Agnes Nicole Sapenne Delisle, worked as a censor during the second world war in Bermuda, Canada and Trinidad. I remember her as a large unmarried lady of imposing appearance, who used to come and have cocktails with my parents at our house in Port of Spain.

Their second child was Kathleen Monica Winifred Delisle, and she married Basil Berridge Davis, mentioned earlier. Their third child, another girl, was Veronica Adele Delisle, know as Anne, and she married 'Chips' Pearce. I also remember the Pearces in war-time Trinidad. They had three daughters, the youngest of whom was called 'Tuppence', I don't know why.

The fourth and last child was another Emile Sapenne Delisle, who inherited the family firm. He and his wife Mildred Jullion, daughter of the Archdeacon of St Kitts, were close friends of my parents, and I grew up with their children,

Peter and Barbara, in St Kitts. Peter's full name, not surprisingly, was Gustave Peter Sapenne Delisle. He lives with his wife Priscilla in Berkshire. Barbara married a South African and died, tragically young.

Chapter 14

Dominic Serres, Marine Painter to King George III, Leonard Cheshire VC, Peter Townsend and Hugh Gaitskell

*Famous non-relatives who happen to be on
my family tree*

I share no genes with Group Captain Peter Townsend, who did not marry Princess Margaret, with Group Captain Leonard Cheshire, who won the Victoria Cross in 1944 and founded, after the war, the Cheshire Foundation Homes for the incurably sick, with Dominic Serres, Marine Painter to King George III, or with Hugh Gaitskell. But they are on my family tree; they are connected by marriage. Not as closely connected as the leg bone with the knee bone or the knee bone with the thigh bone, but connected nevertheless.

And it is the discovering and proving of connections like this that is a large part of the joy of genealogy.

The Serres relations
My grandmother's youngest brother, Edmund Burt, who emigrated to Canada, married Beatrice (Tiny) Boon, who was the daughter of Charles Henry Boon, a man of many parts: doctor, foundryman, newspaper publisher and farmer. His wife was Emily Maria Serres. Emily's great-great-grandfather was the famous artist Dominic Serres RA.

Born in France and brought to England as a prisoner of war, Serres became the artist most sought after to record the epic naval battles of the 18th century. He was elected as a founder member of the Royal Academy in 1768 and was its only marine painter. In 1780 he was appointed Marine Painter to King George III. According to Alan Russett in his lavishly illustrated book *Dominic Serres RA -- 1719-1793 -- War Artist to the Navy*, he was 'the leading marine painter of his time and a significant figure in the art history of the period'.

Dominic's two sons were also artists. Dominique Michael Serres was a landscape painter and drawing master who exhibited nine works at the Royal Academy between 1778 and 1804. His elder brother John Thomas Serres succeeded his father as Marine Painter to the King in 1793 and was later appointed Marine Draught-man [sic] to the Board of Admiralty. His wife, Olivia, also known as Princess Olive of Cumberland, claimed to be the daughter of Henry Frederick, Duke of Cumberland and Strathearn, brother of King George III.

In 1817 she petitioned the king, alleging that she was the daughter of the

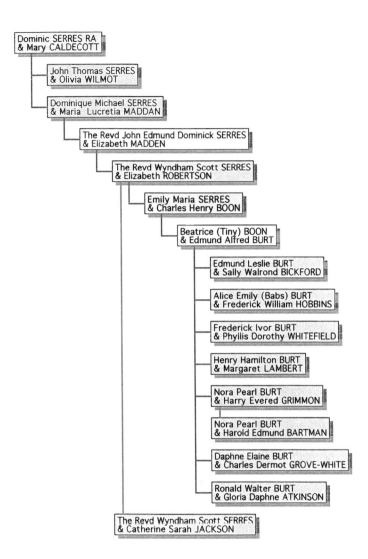

Dominic SERRES RA
& Mary CALDECOTT

John Thomas SERRES
& Olivia WILMOT

Dominique Michael SERRES
& Maria Lucretia MADDAN

The Revd John Edmund Dominick SERRES
& Elizabeth MADDEN

The Revd Wyndham Scott SERRES
& Elizabeth ROBERTSON

Emily Maria SERRES
& Charles Henry BOON

Beatrice (Tiny) BOON
& Edmund Alfred BURT

Edmund Leslie BURT
& Sally Walrond BICKFORD

Alice Emily (Babs) BURT
& Frederick William HOBBINS

Frederick Ivor BURT
& Phyllis Dorothy WHITEFIELD

Henry Hamilton BURT
& Margaret LAMBERT

Nora Pearl BURT
& Harry Evered GRIMMON

Nora Pearl BURT
& Harold Edmund BARTMAN

Daphne Elaine BURT
& Charles Dermot GROVE-WHITE

Ronald Walter BURT
& Gloria Daphne ATKINSON

The Revd Wyndham Scott SERRES
& Catherine Sarah JACKSON

duke by Mrs Payne, a sister of her uncle Dr James Wilmot and the wife of a
naval captain. In 1820, after the death of George III, she asserted herself to be
the legitimate daughter of the Duke of Cumberland and, in a memorial to
George IV, assumed the title of Princess Olive of Cumberland. She hired a
carriage, placed the royal arms on it and drove out with her servants dressed in
royal livery.

According to her story, Dr Wilmot secretly married a sister of King Stanislas

of Poland and had by her a daughter, who was placed under the care of Dr
Wilmot's sister, Mrs Payne. At the age of 18 the girl won the admiration of
both the Duke of Cumberland and the Earl of Warwick, but the earl gave way,
and the duke married her at Lord Archer's house in London on 4 March 1767.
Of this marrage, Olivia claimed to be the child and that ten days after her birth
she was substituted for a stillborn daughter of Dr Wilmot's brother Robert,
who was thenceforth reputed to be her father.

In July 1821 Mrs Serres was arrested for debt and moved the court for a stay
of proceedings on the grounds that she was the legitimate daughter of the Duke
of Cumberland and as such was exempt from arrest in civil cases. But the court
ruled that, as she had put in bail, she was too late to raise the question of privi-
lege. She then produced what purported to be an early will of George III,
leaving £15,000 to 'Olive, the daughter of our brother of Cumberland'. In
1882 she applied to the prerogative court for process to call upon the King's
Proctor to see George III's will, but the court held that it had no jurisdiction.

In 1823 Sir Gerald Noel, who had long interested himself in Mrs Serres'
pretensions, presented a petition to Parliament from 'the Princess of Cumberland'. When he moved that it should be referred to a select committee, the
motion was seconded by Joseph Hume, the radical politician, but Sir Robert
Peel, the Home Secretary, declared Mrs Serres' contentions to be baseless, and
the motion was negatived without a division.

Although separated from her husband ten years earlier, she continued to
aggravate him, endanger his finances and blight his chances of royal prefer-
ment. In 1825 John Thomas Serres died an undischarged debtor. In 1834 Mrs
Serres died, also an undischarged bankrupt.

From painters to clergymen. Dominique Michael Serres' first-born was the
Revd John Edmund Dominick Serres, vicar of St Mary's, Eastbourne. And *his*
first-born was the Revd Wyndham Scott Serres, who went out to Jamaica to be
chaplain at the Kingston Penitentiary and later became rector of St James's,
Nevis. And *his* daughter Emily Maria married Charles Henry Boon, who was
Edmund Burt's father-in-law.

Leonard Cheshire, Peter Townsend and Hugh Gaitskell

My great-grandfather Frederick Augustus Burt (1840-1912) had a younger
brother, Edmund Wigley Burt (1846-1926), one of the seafaring Burts. And
Edmund married Clara Harriet Cook. Clara's father, Edwin Cook, was the
youngest of six brothers. Edwin's brother Charles and his wife Clara had a son
called Arthur, and Arthur had a daughter called Clara (this is the third Clara in
one short paragraph), who married a Cheshire.

Their son Geoffrey was the father of Leonard Cheshire VC.

Another of the Cook brothers, George, complicated matters by changing his
name to Hatt-Cook, in order to perpetuate his mother Isabella's maiden name,

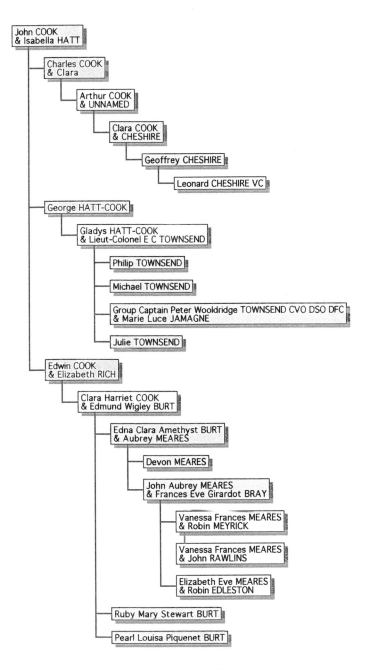

John COOK
& Isabella HATT

Charles COOK
& Clara

Arthur COOK
& UNNAMED

Clara COOK
& CHESHIRE

Geoffrey CHESHIRE

Leonard CHESHIRE VC

George HATT-COOK

Gladys HATT-COOK
& Lieut-Colonel E C TOWNSEND

Philip TOWNSEND

Michael TOWNSEND

Group Captain Peter Wooldridge TOWNSEND CVO DSO DFC
& Marie Luce JAMAGNE

Julie TOWNSEND

Edwin COOK
& Elizabeth RICH

Clara Harriet COOK
& Edmund Wigley BURT

Edna Clara Amethyst BURT
& Aubrey MEARES

Devon MEARES

John Aubrey MEARES
& Frances Eve Girardot BRAY

Vanessa Frances MEARES
& Robin MEYRICK

Vanessa Frances MEARES
& John RAWLINS

Elizabeth Eve MEARES
& Robin EDLESTON

Ruby Mary Stewart BURT

Pearl Louisa Piquenet BURT

rather as Thomas Berkeley Hardtman changed his to Thomas Berkeley Hardt-man Berkeley.

George's daughter Gladys married a Townsend, and they had a son called Peter. He, I had always understood, was the Group Captain with whom Princess Margaret fell in love. But, at this point in writing this book, doubt suddenly struck me. How did I know that it was the same Peter Townsend? What was the evidence? Who, if anyone, had told me? I could not remember.

In genealogical research it is sometimes easy but always dangerous to make assumptions. Further research was clearly called for.

According to *Who's Who*, the Peter Townsend wrote an autobiography called *Time and Chance*, and that, I hoped, would contain some clues. Sure enough, there were no less than 14 references to his mother in the book but not one gave her maiden name! However, her first name was Gladys, and the Peter Townsend had two brothers called Michael and Philip, just like my family tree. In addition, the Peter Townsend had a sister Juliet, while the Peter Townsend on my tree had a sister Julie.

So it seems very likely that the two Peter Townsends were one and the same, and I am proceeding on that basis, although a little more research would not go amiss.

Peter Townsend's godmother was his mother's cousin, Addie Gaitskell, and Cousin Addie had a son called Hugh who was leader of the Labour Party from 1955 until his untimely death in 1963. In 1956 he led the Labour Party in bitter opposition to Prime Minister Eden's aggression against Egypt. As I write this, Labour Prime Minister Blair has sent British troops to invade Iraq. Tony Blair, I am glad to say, is not on my family tree.

The full Birch and Burt family trees are on the internet at
http://mysite.freeserve.com/chris.birch
and http://mysite.freeserve.com/chris.birch/burt *respectively*

Bibliography

Arnold, C T, *Wimbledon National Schools, 1773-1912*, 1912

Bennett, J M, *Sir Archibald Burt, First Chief Justice of Western Australia 1861 - 1879*, The Federation Press, New South Wales, 2002

Branson, Eileen, *History of the Communist Party of Great Britain, 1927-1941*, Lawrence & Wishart, 1985

Branson, Eileen, *History of the Communist Party of Great Britain, 1941-1951*, Lawrence & Wishart, 1997

Buckley, Roger Norman, *Slaves in Red Coats: The British West India Regiments, 1795-1815*, Yale University Press, 1979

Burdon, Katharine Janet, *A Handbook of St Kitts-Nevis*, The West India Committee, London, 1920

Burke, John, *Dictionary of the Landed Gentry of Great Britain and Ireland*, volume II, 1846

Burns, Sir Alan, *Colonial Civil Servant*, George Allen & Unwin, 1949

Burns, Sir Alan, *History of the British West Indies*, George Allen & Unwin, 1954

Burt, Edward, *The Hurricane: A Poem*, C Clark, 1844

Callaghan, John, *Rajani Palme Dutt: A Study in British Stalinism*, Lawrence & Wishart, 1993

Carter, Miranda, *Anthony Blunt: His Lives*, Macmillan, 2001

David, Saul, *Prince of Pleasure*, Little, Brown and Company, 1998

Davis, Gladys, *Three Generations*, published privately

Deacon, Richard, *The Cambridge Apostles: A history of Cambridge University's elite intellectual secret society*, Robert Royce, 1985

Drew, John H, *Remember Kenilworth*, Barracuda Books, 1984

Edwards, Bryan, *The History, Civil and Commercial, of the British Colonies in the West Indies: in Two Volumes*, John Stockdale, 1793

Grimstone, A V (editor), *Pembroke College, Cambridge, A Celebration*, Pembroke College, Cambridge, 1997

Hamshere, Cyril, *The British in the Caribbean*, Weidenfeld and Nicolson, 1972

Hicks, Margery, *Young, Yesterday*, Wordens of Cornwall, 1969

Hobsbawm, Eric, *Interesting Times: A Twentieth-Century Life*, Allen Lane, 2002

Hubbard, Vincent K, *Swords, Ships and Sugar: A History of Nevis to 1900*, Premiere Editions, Placentia, California, 1993

Inniss, Sir Probyn, *Historic Basseterre, The Story of a West Indian Town*, Antigua Printing & Publishing, 1985

King, Francis, and Matthews, George (editors), *About Turn: The British Communist Party and the Second World War*, Lawrence & Wishart, 1990

King, G H, *The Gibraltar of the West Indies: A Chapter from British Imperial History*, The West India Committee, London, 1929

Klugmann, James, *History of the Communist Party of Great Britain: Formation and early years, 1919-1924*, Lawrence & Wishart, 1968

Klugmann, James, *History of the Communist Party of Great Britain: The General Strike, 1925-1926*, Lawrence & Wishart, 1969

Morling, Loreley A, *The Burt Family in Western Australia 1861 - 1994*, Genealogical & Historical Research, Swan View, Western Australia, 1995

Morris, Susan, *The Burt Family*, Debrett Ancestry Research, 1995

Oliver, Vere Langford (editor), *Caribbeana*, volumes 1-6, 1910-1919

Oliver, Vere Langford, *History of the Island of Antigua*, volumes 1-3, 1894-1899

Rector of Colton, *Some Account of Colton and of the De Wasteneys Family*, Houghton & Hammond, 1879

Russett, Alan, *Dominic Serres RA, War Artist to the Navy*, Antique Collectors' Club, 2001

Simpson, D H, *Maria Fitzherbert and Robert Burt, Vicar of Twickenham*, Borough of Twickenham Local History Society, 1974

Soames, Mary (editor), *Speaking for Themselves: The Personal Letters of Winston and Clementine Churchill*, Doubleday, 1998

Tanner, Lawrence, *Recollections of a Westminster Antiquary*, John Baker, 1969

Townsend, Peter, *Time and Chance: An Autobiography*, Collins, 1978

Sunley, Harry, *A Kenilworth Chronology*, Odibourne Press, 1989.

Walker, G P J, *Strings and Pipe: The Story of the Building of an Organ in the Parish Church of St George in the Island of St Kitts in the West Indies in the Year 1872*, St Kitts, 1987

Walmsley, Anne, *The Caribbean Artists Movement 1966-1972*, New Beacon Books, 1992

Whitton, Lieut-Colonel Frederick Ernest, *Moltke*, Constable, 1921

Williams, A, *Sketches in and around Lichfield and Rugeley*, Eggington & Brown and H J Pascoe, 1892

Wood, Neal, *Communism and British Intellectuals*, Victor Gollancz, 1959

Index

As this is a book about genealogy, women's names have been indexed under their maiden names, whenever these are known, with their married names in parentheses. The personal pronoun I, representing the author, appears frequently throughout the book but has been indexed sparingly.

British Council 40 42
Brittan, Leon, Lord 39
Bromley, Antony 38
Browne, James 79
Browne, Jeremiah 79
Brunias, Agostino 45
Bryan, Charles Caines 104 106
Bryan, Emily Verplank (King) 37 59 104
Bryan, John, Dr 70
Bryan, Louisa Emily 70
Buonarotti, Michelangelo 47
Burnham, Forbes 41
Burns, Agnes 115
Burns, Alan Cuthbert Maxwell, Sir 112 114
Burns, Cecil Delisle 112
Burns, Emile 113-115
Burns, James 112 115
Burns, Maurice 115
Burns, Patrick 112
Burns, Robert 115
Burt, Adeline Hamilton (Walwyn) 64 67 117 123 125
Burt, Alfred Earle 70 73
Burt, Alice Louisa 63 64 69 125
Burt, Anna Louisa (Davis) 75 117
Burt, Anne 78
Burt, Anne Mathew (Hutchinson) 123
Burt, Archibald Paull, Sir 69-75 117
Burt, Archibald Piguenit 69 70 73
Burt, Bertha Marie Wilhelmine (Moltke) 87
Burt, Charles Pym (the first) 77 78 84 85
Burt, Charles Pym (1726-1788) 79 85 87
Burt coat of arms 75
Burt, Codrington 78 110
Burt, Daniel Mathew (Grainger) 85
Burt, Daphne Elaine (Grove-White) 64 69
Burt, Donald Irving 64
Burt, Dorcas 81
Burt, Edmund Alfred 67 69 117 130 132

Burt, Edmund Leslie 67
Burt, Edmund Wigley, Captain 70 73 88 132
Burt, Edna Clara Amethyst (Meares) 88
Burt, Edward Musgrave 70
Burt, Edward, Commander 87 88
Burt, Eliza Pitcher (Wigley) 75
Burt, Elizabeth (b 1669) 81
Burt, Elizabeth (b 1734) 77
Burt, Elizabeth (Cumberland) 88
Burt, Elizabeth (Earle) 110 111
Burt, Elizabeth (Fox) 78 79
Burt, Emily Hamilton 52 63 64 66 69 70 98 125
Burt, Fanny (Trollope) 88
Burt, Frances 78
Burt, Francis Sinclair 70 73
Burt, Francis Theodore Page, Sir 38 63 73
Burt, Frederick Archibald 65
Burt, Frederick Augustus 67 69 70 73 75 132
Burt, Frederick Ivor 64 67
Burt, George Henry (1787-1851) 71 74-76 89 111 125
Burt, George Henry (1809-1846) 75
Burt, George Henry (1837-1867) 70 73 75
Burt, George Henry (1862-1864) 75
Burt, Gertrude Aimee (Johnson) 65
Burt, Helena Maud 65 69 75
Burt, Ingeborg Mabel (Gordon) 64 65 125
Burt, James 77
Burt, Jane 78
Burt, John Heyliger 87
Burt, John Musgrave 70
Burt, Leonard Archibald 65
Burt, Lilian Mary (King) 2 4 17 18 33 36-38 50 51 54 63 67 125
Burt, Louisa Emily (Leake) 70 73
Burt, Mary (Weekes) 78
Burt, Mina Eliza (Fraser) 70 73
Burt, Nora Pearl (Grimmon, Bartman) 67

Davis, Benjamin Shuttleworth 98 117
118-121 123
Davis coat of arms 117
Davis, Constance Gwendolyn 121
Davis, Constance Margaret (Forbes)
121
Davis, Daniel Gateward, The Rt Revd
70
Davis, Doris Ismay (Jones) 123
Davis, Emma Agnes Darnell (Davis)
119 120
Davis, Gillian Valentine (Vaughan) 122
Davis, Gladys Darnell (Betty) 98 121
122
Davis, John, Colonel (d 1725) 117
Davis, John (1728-1794) 117
Davis, John Nicholas 117
Davis, Kathleen Doris Therese
(Walwyn) 117 122 123 126
Davis, Pamela Kathleen (Cogan) 122
Davis, Robert Leslie 121
Davis, Steuart Arthur Hamilton 120
121
Davis, Steuart Darnell Spencer 120
121
Davis, Steuart Spencer 75 117 120
Davis, (Steuart) Spencer, Sir 119 120
Davis, Tania Ann (Platts) 120 121
Davis, William (the first) 117
Davis, William (the second) 117
Davis, William (the third) 117
Davis, William Berridge 121
Davis, William Darnell 117
Debrett Ancestry Research Ltd 79
Delisle, Agnes (Burns) 112 115 127
Delisle, Agnes Nicole Sapenne 128
Delisle, Antoine 126
Delisle, Barbara 128 129
Delisle, Emile Sapenne (the first) 112
114 126
Delisle, Emile S (the second) 126
Delisle, Emile Sapenne (the third) 126
128
Delisle, Gustave Peter Sapenne 128 129
Delisle, Gustave (d 1918) 117 126
Delisle, Kathleen Monica Winifred

(Davis) 117 123 128
Delisle, Margerite Rosatie Sapenne
(Thurston) 115 126 127
Delisle, Priscilla 129
Delisle, Sydney 51
Delisle, Veronica Adele (Pearce) 128
Democrat, The 47 48
Digby, Hildegarde (Berkeley), Mrs
107
Dollman, Mr 93
Douglas, Frances Pym 79
Douglas, John 79
Douglas-Home, Alec, Sir 108
Doyle, Arthur Conan, Sir 1
Duke of York's Royal Canadian Hussars 50
Duport, Hester (Burt) 87
Dutt, Rajani Palme 114 115

Earle, Barbara Haliburton Margaret
111
Earle, Charles John 111
Earle, Edward (1673-1728) 110
Earle, Edward, Colonel 110
Earle, Geoge 110
Earle, John (1722-1771) 110
Earle, John (1748-1807) 110 111
Earle, Mary (Berkeley) 37 110
Earle, Mary Elizabeth 111
Earle, Roger, Captain 110
Earle, Samuel 110
Earle, Sarah (McTair) 111
Eden, Anthony, Earl of Avon 134
Elm Grove Baptist Chapel 10
Ellis, Annie 31 32
Ellis, Fanny 31
Ellis, Jane 31
Ellis, John 31 32
Ellis, S 31
Emms, Arthur Edward 20 21
Emms, Miriam Jeanette 19 20
Emms, Violet 21
Emra, Lucy (Earle) 111
Enfield, Elinor (Burns) 115

Fabian Society 114
Farrow's Bank 1

Fitzallan-Howard, Sarah Margaret
(Clutton), Lady 19
Fitzherbert, Maria, Mrs 86 87
Forbes, Alastair Granville, Sir 122
Forbes, Granville 121
Foreman, Lillian Agnes (Burt) 65
Fortescue, Earl 96
Fowler, Mary (Searle) 98 99
Foxall, Anne Elizabeth (Gregory) 27-
29
Franco, Francisco, General 114
Frank, John 80
Fred 9

Gaitskell, Addie 134
Gaitskell, Hugh Todd Naylor 130 132
134
Garibaldi, Giuseppe 23
Garland, Charles 14 24
Garland, Elizabeth 23
Garland, Ellen (Birch) 12 14-17 19 22 24
Garland, James 24
Garland, John 23
Garland, Sarah Shrimpton (Lissolo)
22 23
Garland, William, Captain 22-24
Garman, Gwenneth Mary (Bradley)
17 19
Garman, William Edwin 17
General Life & Fire Office 10
General Life Assurance Company 10
Georgian House 47
Gibbs, Oswald 45
Gibson, Evelyn 50
Gilbert, Harriette (Gregory) 30
Gilbert, John (1829-1907) 30
Gilbert, John (Harriette's father) 30 Glasgow
University 112
Goddard, Rayner, Lord 38
Godfrey, Dan, Sir 30
Gordon, Violet Woodley (Wiggins)
65
Grainger, James, Dr 85
Grasse, Count de 56
Gray's Inn 38
Gray, Thomas 41

Gregory, Alice Mary 25
Gregory, Ann 29
Gregory, Christopher Washington 28
Gregory, Derek Peyton 25
Gregory, Edith Vera (Collinson) 25
Gregory, Frederick Peyton 25
Gregory, George Peyton 10 25-31
Gregory, Harriette Elizabeth (Birch) 2
9 10 21 22 25 26 29
Gregory, James (1758-1817) 29
Gregory, James (1791-1873) 25 27-29
Gregory, James Pemberton 28
Gregory, Jane Kate 25
Gregory, Joshua 29
Gregory, Julian John 25
Gregory, Rosena Annie 25 26
Gregory, Rosena Sarah Anne
(Pinhorn) 27
Gregory, Sarah 29
Gregory, William Frederick 25
Gregory, William Jabez 28
Grinlington, Colonel 8
Grinlington, Mrs 8

Hall School, Wincanton 21
Halley, Edmund 33
Hammond, Mary (Walwyn) 126
Hardtman, Elaine Bertha Hamilton
(Davis) 121
Hardtman, Helen Marjorie Berkeley
(Holmes a Court, Walwyn) 126
Hardtman, Thomas Allman 106
Hardtman, Thomas Berkeley 106 107
121 134
Harris, Henry James 19
Harris, James 12
Harris, Walter Brittan 19
Hatt, Isabella 132
Hatt-Cook, George 132 134
Hatt-Cook, Gladys (Townsend) 134
Hawker, Rear-Admiral E 87
Hawkes, Sam 79
Haynes, Antony 46
Heller, Joseph 72
Hemert, Anna van (Burt) 87
Hess, Myra, Dame 21

Pembroke College Cambridge Society *Annual Gazette* 39 45
Perrillier, Zulma (Delisle) 126
Peyton, George 29 30
Piguenit, Anne 90
Piguenit, Frederick 90
Piguenit, Haidee Irene (Lacy-Hulbert) 90
Piguenit, James 90
Piguenit, James George 89 90
Piguenit, James George Burt 90
Piguenit, Samuel 89 90
Piguenit, William Charles 90
Pitt, David Thomas, Lord 41 48
Pitt, William (the Younger) 27 41
Poincy, Phillipe de 47
Pollitt, Harry 114 115
Powell, John Enoch, The Rt Hon 39
Power, Robert 99
Princess Margaret 134
Princess Olive of Cumberland 130-132
Prince Alfred, Duke of Edinburgh 94
Prince Consort 16
Prince of Wales 16 86 87
Public Record Office 40 59
Pym, Charles, Captain (d 1741) 79
Pym, Charles, Colonel (1650-1699) 79
Pym, Elizabeth (Burt) 77-79
Pym, Jane (Burt) 79
Pym, Priscilla (Marsham) 79
Pym, Thomas 79 81

Queen Adelaide 16
Queen Elizabeth II 48
Queen Elizabeth the Queen Mother 91 121
Queen Victoria 16 29 52 94

Radcliffe, George, The Revd 92
Ramsey, Kenneth 44
Rattenbury Arnold 115
Rawlins, Anne (Walwyn) 123
Rawlins, Elizabeth 123
Rawlins, Henry 123
Rawlins, Joseph 123

Redford, Mary (Scargill) 99 101
Redford, Mr 99 101
Regent's Park Zoo 17
Reid, Marjorie (Lady Wigley) 35
Religious Society of Friends 21
Ridler, Patricia Ethel (Manning) 12
Riley, Richie 42
Robertson, Hector Harold 6 7
Rodney, George Brydges, Lord 56
Rogers, Alice (Birch) 12
Rose, La, John 43
Rose, Elizabeth Ann (Birch) 9 17 18 22
Rougier, Mr Justice 43
Rowe, J W F 40
Royal Academy 7 130
Royal Air Force 35
Royal Bank of Canada 34
Royal Canadian Mounted Police 17
Royal College of Music 21
Royal Commonwealth Society 43
Royal Corsican Rangers 23
Russett, Alan 130
Ryan, Edward 48
Rylands, John Paul 99

Salkey, Andrew 43
Salvation Army 121
Sanders, Jane (Savery) 62
Sanders, Margaret Jane (Savery) 62
Savery, Jane Sanders Pooler (King) 60 62
Savery, John (the elder) 60 61
Savery, John (junior) 61
Savery, John Alexander 60 62
Savery, Mary Ann (Thomas) 60
Scargill, John 93 98 99 101
School House, Wimbledon 27
Schroeder, Miss 27 29
Searle, Charles Edward, Dr 97-99
Searle, C W A, Dr 98
Serres, Dominic 130
Serres, Dominique Michael 130
Serres, Emily Maria (Boon) 130 132
Serres, John Edmund Dominic, The Revd 132

Walwyn, Joy 126
Walwyn, Kathleen Berkeley Mary
    (Wiggins) 65
Walwyn, Keith Lynnington 40 51 125
Walwyn, Daphne Lilian (Boyce) 67
    125
Walwyn, Philip 125
Walwyn, Thomas 123
Walwyn, William 123
Walwyn, William Earle Llewellyn
    123 125 126
Warder, Rebecca Jane (Birch) 19 20
Warner, Thomas, Sir 47 55 78
Warner Park 54 54 59
Warwick, Earl of 132
Waterloo, Battle of 22-24
Waterloo Box 22 24
Weatherill, Charles Pym 79
Weatherill, James 79
Webb, Beatrice 114
Weekes, Ivan 41
Wellington, Arthur Wellesley, Duke
    of 23
Weslyan Sunday School 9
Westminster Abbey 44 45
West Cumberland Hospital 36
West India Committee 40 56
West Indian Students Centre 42 45
White Thorn House 12
Wiggins, Bruce Gordon 65 125
Wiggins, Edmund Earle 65
Wigley, Francis Spencer 70 75
Wigley, John Leslie, Captain 125
Wigley, Wilfred, Sir 35
Willet, John 79
Willson, Idonia (Delisle) 128
Wilmot, James, Dr 131 132
Wilmot, Olive (Payne) 131 132
Wilmot, Olivia (Serres) 130-132
Wilmot, Robert 132
Wimbledon Free School 27 28
Women's Army Auxiliary Corps 6
Women's Voluntary Service 35
Wood, Catherine Mary (Burt) 86
Wood, Henry Joseph, Sir 20 21
Woodward, Ann (Ellis) 31

Woodward, Elizabeth (Gilbert) 31 32
Woodward, Harriet 31
Woodward, Jane (Badford) 31
Woolley, Rebekah (Burt) 77